# TRUST IN TRASH

by Karen Kellock Ph.D.

---

## Manual for
## Superior Men

**A complete theory based on Einstein physics,
Political Psychology, Systems Theory
and Archetypal Psychiatry.**

**FORMULA**

**All success attraction
All disease obstruction
All recovery elimination**

**You must fast on all three**

**OBSTRUCTIONS:**

**People
Habit
Food**

# TRUST IN TRASH

**Narcissistic relationships are tornados: they sweep us off our feet and we forget who we are.    A true emotional cutoff dissolves your symptoms. If still hooked they will persist cuz it's a system.    It is frightening the bad decisions made to get each other's approval--these women need removal.    If you live for their approval you'll die by their rejection--you're so much happier never thinking about em.**

# TRUST IN TRASH

MY GOD THEY SLAPPED ME AROUND
PUBLIC HUMILIATION
HOMEOSTASIS ALWAYS
THERE CAN BE NO FORGIVENESS
COMPENSATORY CALUMNY
HIGH VALUE WOMEN
DRIVEN MAD BY OPINIONS OF OTHERS
THE IRRELEVANCE OF OPINIONS
HOW TO RID PAST MEMORIES
NO QUEEN WOULD EVER CHASE
THEY WANNA TAKE OVER HOMES
NO INSULT STAYS IN HER MIND
OWNING YOUR HIGH DESTINY
GENERATION OF BROKEN CONSCIOUSNESS
DON'T BE CHEAP
WOMEN WHO CHASE MEN
FIRED BY DESPERATION
DIVERSE LUSTS OF PURSUING WOMEN
COVERT NARCISSISM
COLD, ALOOF, AVOIDANT
IT'S YOUR FAULT
PASSIVE-AGGRESSIVE COVERT TYPE
WOMEN GOING BAD
FEMALE DEMONS/REPENTANCE
RECIPE FOR BEDLAM
SUM COST FALLACY
THE CONTAGION OF MADNESS
THE ARCHETYPES
THE FIFTIES WERE LOW KEY
DUNNING KRUGER AND SEX
REPERCUSSIONS OF BEING CHEAP
SPIRIT OF DISHONOR
GOSSIP, CALUMNY AND LITTLE MINDS
LIVE RIGHT/GOD TAKES EM OUT
STAY A LEGEND
NEVER CHASE A MAN, LET HIM WIN YOU
FEMINIST MAD PURSUIT

# TRUST IN TRASH

WOMAN THE GLORY OF MAN
THREE TYPES OF MEN
REPORTED FOR BEI BEING SINGLE SUX
THE THRILL WILL BE GONE
TRAUMATIZED FEMALE DEVILS
NG DIFFERENT
YOU HURT ME, I'M DONE SEE
BALANCE OF POWER
ALL CYCLES HAVE AN END
SEX BASED ON PRECEDENT
TURNING FAMILY MEMBERS AGAINST YOU
NARCISSISTIC SUPPLY
SUDDENLY THEY HATE YOU
EMOTIONAL CUTOFF DISSOLVES SYMPTOMS
THINKING IS VERBOTEN
HE'S JEALOUS OF YOUR THOUGHTS
MUST GO NO CONTACT
NON-VERBAL IS IT
SELF-COMPASSION IS THE GOAL
LEVELING
REPUBLICAN PUSSIES
BIG BLACK CLOUD OF SILENT HATREDS
MICRO-CHEATING
PRESENT ONLY YOUR SELF
THE RECOVERED LADY SAID
HOOK UP TO GET BACK
PROMISCUITY MAKES YOU UGLY
LURING AND BAITING
AGELESS CORNUCOPIA VS. BULLIES
BULLIES ARE ABOUT NARCISSISM
BULLIES POWERFUL IN CREATING DESTRUCTION
MUST WATCH TEEN BULLIES
BULLY SUE WANTS DEPENDENCY
EITHER LEAD (GAIN RESPECT) OR BE SLAIN
UNIQUE SEED POTENTIALS BLOSSOM WITH REPENTANCE
DEMOCRATS ARE GLOBALISTS
REPENTANCE: BEING CARRIED DOWNSTREAM

# TRUST IN TRASH

TRASH IS CHAOTIC CLUTTER
ARISTOCRATIC NEATNESS
THE BLIND DON'T FEEL SLIGHTS
SICK ATTACHMENTS-THRU-DENIAL
CAREFUL WHO YOU ASSOCIATE WITH
KEEP CHATTERERS AT BAY
DETACH: NOW *GOD* DEFINES YOU
SEE IT THEN RELEASE IT
NO FRIENDS = SUCCESS
GETTING HURT BY WRONG PEOPLE
DETACH FROM OUTER, IMPLODE TO INNER
THE NICE LADY IS REALLY A SCORPION
HOLD YOUR HEAD UP HIGH
CRUELIANS EXCUSE BRUTALITY
THEY EXPLODE WITH POLITE CRUELTIES
DETACH, THERE'S NOTHING THEY CAN DO
THEY BLOCKED YOUR FASCINATION
HOME CENTER:  SOLITUDE
A BLANK SLATE FOR OTHER'S PROJECTIONS
STAY HOME AND CHOOSE YOUR EXPERIENCE
SEPARATE/INSULATE TO REFLECT GOD
CRUELIANS HAVE NO COMPASSION
WELCOME TO A PEACEFUL VIEW
SPIRITUAL GIFTS GONE WITH THE RIFTS
HEALTH UPDATES
STAY SWEET,  KEEP SWEET
INTUITION SAYS FRUIT IS SAFE
FROM FAT TO STARCH REVERSALS
DROP PLANT FATS FOR AWHILE
THO' A FRUIT, AVO'S A FAT
UNDERCARBED INSECURITY IS UGLY
SPIN DOCTORS AND PLASTIC SURGEONS
HOW TO RID JUNK AND REMORSE
GENIUS AND CATNAPS
CLIMATE ALARMISM IS COMMUNISM
SYSTEM BASIS OF INSANITY
WAIT FOR THE GREAT DIVIDE

# TRASH NOTES

## OUR JOB:  GET THEM READY

The job of the older woman is to educate the younger to stop doing what's dragging her under.

Even children made fun of Beethoven. All great geniuses have this constantly happenin'.

Constant abusive torment can make you like firm steel or a whimpering weak weasel, it's up to you.

If you wake up bad, recall God doesn't want us sad or mad so who's influencing your head?

There's a thing called Moral Insanity although of course you wouldn't hear of this today.

## JUSTICE IS NECESSARY FOR RELIEF

Justice is necessary for the relief of the saints and at this time that's all I gotta say.

When asking for justice ask yourself: What would Lucas McCain do? I always think about this.

Promiscuous men aren't the best lovers but the worst, because you're a haunted house sir.

Evil helpers: Good riddance, pay them off. Keep em happy as they leave then just thank God.

When you reject em be nice and courteous because these days dumped people show violence.

What fame should mean: chance to make an amazing new dent, a bully pulpit to teach or vent.

# TRASH NOTES

Your enemies are dead, gone or in a rest home so why can't you let grudges go from long ago?

**WOMEN, GROW UP!**

To hear women in their seventies swearing and going to wet T-shirt contests is truly sickening.

Women got more decent with age but these days to copy youth they get more immoral ok.

It's insane, getting boob jobs in their sixties then in the rest home two big udders blocking thee.

Restored old paths, that should be the goal. For the present era is insane and getting old.

Elder females: it's your job to educate the youth not cave into them and be equally uncouth.

It's the awful, horrible and embarrassing incidents that made me who I am today, thanks.

Since the narcissist's number one tactic is lovebombing we must prepare the traumatized queen.

**GOD PURIFIES THE PAST**

The bad eras of your life may contain a pearl of exciting wisdom for the future tho' it was strife.

Bad eras may be perceived thru others' lens and thus it's a false view and very bad for us.

The era causing most friction/commotion: because you're expressing your inner kingdom?

No matter what "they" say God reads the intention of your heart and enemies will pay.

What you went thru was so bad even thinking about it causes anxiety: welcome to the club.

# TRASH NOTES

They hounded/humiliated me until my world lost all logic then I cried to Thee and You saved me.

Live it up, you only live once. I hope you don't lose your life or mind, a permanent dunce.

When the hedge is down it's like God lets things happen: we were that unteachable until then.

Old grudges: remember you were both younger then, maybe both immature and it was a system.

God purifies the past so lets try for good memories now. Work at it: replace thoughts in a row.

When you recall a bad era, think on the good parts of it and replace thoughts etcetera.

## DAILY ROUTINES AND THINGS

High tech trick: how do you fix skin looking like crepe? Anything with ammonium lactate.

Make it all music then life's one big party. Thinking, planning, errands and viewing eternity.

Eat anything you want for the Breakfast Only Plan as long as the rest of the day you fast man.

It's Break-Fast Only, get it? You eat between fasts or from fast to fast [it's so splendid].

Someone gave me a "cookie". it sent me into the galaxy and had to go to emergency, Lord forgive me.

Funny they call it Medical Marijuana because it's so strong the new weed will surely kill ya.

I did all this with no hope of reward except faith in Him, and that's what He'll be rewardin'

# TRUST IN TRASH

It's all HOMEOSTASIS: water maintaining it's own level and in human systems that's the devil.

We're MEANT to take dominion--that's a king or queen--but this consciousness is broken.

Most people say they don't touch a drop but a drop touches them. Stanley in Streetcar

Narcissistic relationships are tornados: they sweep us off our feet/we don't know where we are.

They rationalize their poor behavior by their cognitive distortions seeming normal to them.

When codependent we are other-focused so when it blows up we just naturally go to Self.

The codependent looks outward for validation, losing his power to something he can't control.

Self-control is most important, a spiritual fruit. But if in sin, revealing "autonomisms" come thru.

Good fit: codependent feels fault for everything and narcissist always blames someone else.

What hurt most was being mischaracterized thru slip ups. Self-control is why this stopped.

## MY GOD THEY SLAPPED ME AROUND

My God they slapped me around, showed me who's who/rehashed what the left says too.

I just wanna stay home behind a locked gate with dogs, a molt and machine guns said the sage.

# TRUST IN TRASH

We were weakened thru trauma and the evil world came in like a tidal wave in America.

Write boldly but be as sweet as a kitten for you know what you're up against: the wicked.

People are horrible and the worst are the virtue-signalers and progressive sociables.

We had to accept that liberal crap for years until Trump put our inner resentments into words.

The worst was frenemy girlfriends encouraging us to sin. Good was bad and bad good, amen.

Beta males actually look to their liberal democrat wives for leadership--these are disgusting twits.

## PUBLIC HUMILIATION

A sane reaction to public humiliation is realizing our core decency and right to be loved.

Not only is he a terrorist the narcissist is a public humiliator so stay prayed up/prepared.

He's gonna hurt you, compelled to pull you down/make you a clown. Recall those you've known.

The narcissist's whole thing is chaos to take control and your humiliation plays that role.

He exploits our guilt and who hasn't done something they're not proud of? He milks that.

## HOMEOSTASIS ALWAYS

No matter your achievements he'll make you feel lower than him since it's all about compensation.

# TRUST IN TRASH

He doesn't wanna hear of your achievements today he'll bring up your sins back decades.

Your loving sisters will lay evil seeds wherever you're going then watch your world turn hating.

All of these cruel social devices are compensations for feeling inadequate but so what?

I never went to that dentist again after his invasive officious comments pulling me down.

## THERE CAN BE NO FORGIVENESS

They've grown up conflicted in fear of imminent judgement so you CAN'T be forgiven.

All of life is a hierarchy to them so your slip means your degrade and there's no going on ahead.

They're afraid of public shame so they compensate by avoiding guilt and shame at your expense.

The root of "humiliation" is dirt--they're trying to bring you down to DIRT LEVEL, e.g. a dirty girl.

To humiliate: bring injury to one's dignity and self-respect, creating feelings of powerlessness.

Have the narcissists you've known taken you through something. like this? Yes, even your sis.

They must shame you publicly and they always misrepresent--an identity catastrophe.

They publicly expose what THEY think should be your shame, never ever to be forgotten ok.

That's the extent of their morality: to expose YOUR shame, fit for the gallows but not their own.

# TRUST IN TRASH

God told me [when called rotten and censored from talkin'] i'd someday tell what happened.

For those of you who can't relocate after an ordeal like this, I commiserate. Persevere and pray.

## COMPENSATORY CALUMNY

Calumny--soul murder--is killing one's reputation. It's a horrible weapon so pray God'll get em.

When narcissists use humiliation they've turned the relationship into a contest of domination.

I'm gonna dominate you by pulling down your reputation turning you into a public shrew.

Another compensation is overt rudeness and insults, ignoring needs or reasonable requests.

Glares and stares, refusing to acknowledge your physical presence--you don't even exist.

Withholding money, helpfulness or common courteousness. Sudden weirdness and stress.

One way or another his compensatory mechanisms bring you down in a big black cloud.

Mocking your preferences, making fun of your unique interests, colluding with your enemies.

Demean you to make you look foolish, draw constant attention to failures, show obvious favoritism.

They'll demand loyalty and withhold favors until they get it sufficiently, like a gang is run see.

He loves shunning you publicly, making you know you are a **NOBODY** in relation to him especially.

# TRUST IN TRASH

The narcissist does not want people to think well of you at all. He'll joke/mock/deride, it's awful.

## HIGH VALUE WOMEN

Queen consciousness is the high self-concept existing independently of their gossip/comments.

It's the high self esteem that a woman possesses that is independent of anything or anyone.

Where is a woman who never needs the world to esteem her? A ringing phone just bugs her.

Her self-esteem account is self-supplied and self sufficient and that is her distinguishment.

Her self-esteem is so independent she's immune to sour disapproval or negative opinions.

## DRIVEN MAD BY OPINIONS OF OTHERS

Most women are driven MAD by opinions of others but with a queen it's garbage in/garbage out sir.

Whether you agree or disagree with her it's not gonna shake how she feels about anything see.

Queen consciousness is possessing the capacity to own her destiny [future] without timidity.

She never dumbs it all down to become more appealing to the mediocre/undeserving.

But the Queen steps into the whole vision the Creator's given to her--she steps into it with flair.

Embracing a future with faith in your ability: this is the queen or a child of God, pride of divinity.

# TRUST IN TRASH

Queen consciousness is standing alone if needed as a whole person independent of a system.

She's never in a situation where to be whole she needs extra, she's happy with nothing or fiesta.

She's never duped by bad associates see, embracing the grand future with faith in her ability.

Queen conscious women are not obsessing over age but strength within to live life as a sage.

Not obsessing over things she can't control, a queen strategizes over what she can/the flow.

A queen is always growing and laying a foundation for her future not obsessing over you sir.

The inner fortitude to embrace your life and future as an individual tho' marriage is still crucial.

## THE IRRELEVANCE OF OPINIONS

Embracing your OWN truth, being everything God has given you gifts to be, that's the Queen.

Embracing everything that she is, free of ridicule or rejection always with eyes to the horizon.

It's the high self-concept existing independently of other's opinions: truly being content.

Satan gets us thru self-devaluation til we think we're nothing. Get ID thru accomplishing something.

Her self-esteem account is self-supplied and self-sufficient while the others are sycophants.

She's so high even blatant disapproval won't move her, that's the kinda queen you want sir.

# TRUST IN TRASH

Who am I? My routines, affections, past times, interests, hobbies, love of home and family.

A queen does not chart her course based on opinions or approval of others/mental shorts.

A queen never chases/takes a chance on rejection constantly lowering her self-conception.

A woman chasing a man is disgusting. Put this energy into your own destiny and feel lucky.

Most women are driven mad by the opinions of others and I was like this for most of my life sir.

## HOW TO RID PAST MEMORIES

Maybe I'm insane, maybe I'm delaying. Enjoy thy day & do what's in front without complaining.

How to rid past memories: Build up new ones and as projects unfold old relics start dispersing.

One reason for constant remorse over the past is nothing's happening in the present yet.

My God the lowest possible scum would cooperate with these guys, Lord help us please.

A woman can trigger a man's higher intelligence or she can drag him down thru henpeckedness.

A woman may regress thru sensual sins. Since she's supposed to edify this is doubly disgustin'.

We should be derogatory about human nature and how it's degraded for fifty years or more.

Lady said "I've had enough of the passive-aggressive style of self-absorption and control."

# TRUST IN TRASH

I'm the opposite to a fame whore. I wanna stay low, in sweet solitude and beneath the radar.

## NO QUEEN WOULD EVER CHASE

If she chases a man and wins, that's not the kinda man who can lead her into anything but ruin.

So the queen chases him and wins, now he's sitting around the mansion/running her errands.

Never mention it again. Whatever it was has blown over and we're back in synchrony to win.

She sees her increasing "lost value" index and it pushes her into doing the ridiculous.

There's lotsa men who'd like a cushy existence with the mistress who's also a great social hostess.

Do they work, do they create? No they get a place to stay by keeping her neurotic fears away.

When I'm around em I feel all my gears reversing and grinding, wanna go home to my own reality.

Ladies: I'm not losing value I'm gaining it with age and no high value woman would ever chase!

Get into your gifts/talents and home and your homemaking skills alone will attract the one.

## THEY WANNA TAKE OVER HOMES

A queen must plan for her own future and have her own home or it's hell sucking up ya know.

You have a home, I have a home. So what are you always doing here, I just wanna be alone.

# TRUST IN TRASH

They wanna take over homes. Don't let em use you as a bathroom or place to charge their phone.

People are lonely and bored so don't let em use you for entertainment by always coming over.

It's a continual dripping their coming without announcing and it's chaos I'm declaring.

They ain't got nothing going on so use you for entertainment, another sucking spirit.

Get RID of these people, cut em loose. Open to eternity/wide-angled vision without abuse.

I want NO interruptions, ever. That's being a queen, not a sitting duck for the bored gossiper.

Self-control hones skills until it's divinely perfect and self-discipline provides the daily map.

I want NO interruptions in this day of divine synchronicity in eternity as a female homie.

Your mother was a horrible woman. No, she was a saint--she tried to warn me about you.

## NO INSULT STAYS IN HER MIND

No insult stays in your mind and plays with it when you're queen conscious, it all goes out.

The queen possesses the capacity to own her own destiny: she knows why she exists see.

The queen knows where she's going and is not timid about it in fear of obvious jealousy.

All you gotta do is succeed and people are rubbed the wrong way. Do your great thing anyway.

Don't ever cut back to appear more appealing to inferior people though it's tempting to.

To become more appealing they dumb it down but the queen never does this, she's full blown.

She steps into that complete creative vision given by her Creator despite ridicule and derision.

## OWNING YOUR HIGH DESTINY

Owning your destiny is waiting for the RIGHT man not running behind a handy one in desperation.

Esther said, If I perish let me perish but I'm gonna fulfill the destiny my Creator gave me, period.

Queen simply means she has the inner fortitude to embrace life and her future as an individual.

The queen can stand alone when necessary cuz she's whole apart from anyone or anything.

No hankering for relationship cuz she feels incomplete--that never happens to the queen.

She owns her destiny with faith in her ability, never obsessing over age or other identities.

While women are traumatized over things they can't control queens are strategizing what they know.

No spending money to create a false persona to attract a man just being your divine self amen.

The average woman obsesses over relationship then has nothing whatsoever to show for it.

The queen concentrates on what she CAN control: not a man but her own mind & spiritual regimen.

# TRUST IN TRASH

The queen is always growing and laying a foundation for her own future not chasing desire.

## GENERATION OF BROKEN CONSCIOUSNESS

When you've lost your value you slide in with society telling you you're a slave not a ruler see.

Broken queen consciousness tells her she must beg for the value which is already given to her.

Too many women are in hot pursuit of men and it's a definite block to healthy relationships.

Her value drops like a rock being so readily available, that's the trouble with modern females.

It doesn't matter what she's worth, if she does not know her worth she'll surely be cursed.

How the world respects and responds to her will degrade suddenly if she's acting unlovely.

A high value woman gets drunk and has an affair. Her value drops suddenly/they wanna kill her.

## DON'T BE CHEAP

The repercussions of being cheap work on your self-esteem subconsciously = disease.

Knowing this you must never again use sex as dating currency and you must truly mean it honey.

Feminism has ruined women by saying the sex instincts are equal. Everything's equal goes to hell.

You don't owe that man a favor and you need not explain. He's the immoral one for even asking ok.

And should you "slip", one-time sex is no contract to continue--never let a man use you..

Don't get down in the dumps cuz all of us have made mistakes. Sexual ones and others, ok.

You're so busy settling for the surface aspects of a man you never see the substance, it's low man.

You're looking at what he's wearing, what he's driving, where he went to school--his wrappings.

## WOMEN WHO CHASE MEN

Whether you do or not has nothing to do with me, I'm only. concerned with fulfilling my destiny.

When a woman pursues a man it's a pure manifestation of masculine energy-- what a turnoff honey.

A masculine woman in hot pursuit attracts a feminine man but always repels a masculine one.

In pursuing men you'll never attract the type who can truly sustain you, just a couch potato.

A pursuing woman misrepresents her virtue and her desperation sends the wrong signal.

She carries herself showing she is loyal, has balanced emotions and can be trusted as wife.

A desperate female is bleeding in the water, attracting sharks to devour all that's left of her.

## FIRED BY DESPERATION

A woman in pursuit is usually fired by desperation or "lowered Value", a subconscious trigger.

# TRUST IN TRASH

The desperation of increasingly lowered value is a sign to predators who swoop in to flatter her.

Predators pick up on emotional weakness indicated by desperation, it's like a starting gun.

When predators sense emotional weakness they manipulate/manage, they take advantage.

It's now creeping into houses with wicked men leading away captive silly women with sins.

Thru advancing desperation she does things she normally wouldn't do like go to a saloon.

I've had men creep into my life trying to lead me away as if laden with sins/owned by them.

This type of mindset burdens her with sins as she's "crooked" not humming with the universe.

## DIVERSE LUSTS OF PURSUING WOMEN

When chasing a man diverse kinds of lusts accrue since it was never God's plan for a woman.

The day a queen wakes up to lost value and decides to pursue a king is the day she will lose him.

Pursuing a man gets mean for the potential for disapproval shatters a woman's self-esteem.

The woman is not built to sustain rejection whereas a man gets used to it, he's designed for it.

The potential for rejection is way too risky for the woman to step outside of her role see.

The more she pursues while being rejected she is broken, thinking less of herself/forsaken.

# TRUST IN TRASH

Hope deferred makes her heart sick. Every time she strives/pursues and fails she's less slick.

We weren't part of the club of interlocking families with millions of members, we were outsiders.

Never let em in just cuz they want in. Being a good hostess to rascals could be your sin.

## COVERT NARCISSISM

The narcissist is very skilled at creating a groupthink atmosphere where you are the other.

There's no such thing as "no communication" because just that's a giant message of rejection.

The silent language of covert narcissism: I'm gonna show you what I think of you without sayin'

The covert is just as grandiose as the brash narcissist but far more difficult to pin down sis.

The covert is far more under the radar in showing his self-absorption, like being disinterested.

Disinterested, inattentive plus flying monkeys/useful idiots doing their bidding and all the rejecting.

They get together and deem you irrelevant. They snub anything you say no matter how intelligent.

They've low regard for your opinions and zero concern for your well-being, that's groupthink.

## COLD, ALOOF, AVOIDANT

They can be cold, aloof, condescending or avoidant. They can be "forgetful"-- all bull.

They're emotionally unavailable or quietly self-indulgent, you know what I'm talking about.

They can be non-affectionate or give no affirmation, or have an air of sarcasm in conversation.

They can be super-defensive and tho' I know it's an armor they're carrying it's overwhelming.

So yes, the covert narcissist says a helluva lot without using words and knowing that is best.

When they go into their non-communication communication it says "you mean nothing".

His silent behavior says: "I'm the only one in this equation that really matters, can't you see?"

Message clear: Connecting with people takes too much energy, they don't wanna be bothered.

## IT'S YOUR FAULT

It'd be best learning better communicational skills but it's much easier to say "its your fault".

He loves the power he gets from being mysterious, from keeping everything a dam secret.

I just love watching people scramble when I sabotage their good plans says the narcissist man.

"No one, and I mean NO ONE, is gonna tell me what to think, say or do". Covert narcissist

I get a huge thrill when I see how frustrated you feel, it's a big game to me still. Narcissist

I won't tell you a lie but I'm not that committed to honesty ok? That narcissist guy.

# TRUST IN TRASH

The silent language of the covert narcissist must be recognized so mental health is realized.

## PASSIVE-AGGRESSIVE COVERT TYPE

You've had enough of this passive-aggressive covert style of self-absorption and control.

This president embarrassed us all weekend with his forgetfulness, apologies and weakness.

I would put a bee in his bonnet and he'd get right on it. Was I dominant then? No that's not it.

The top IQs in this world are men see and there are no women in that [chest master] league.

Build it and they will come. Just concentrate on your own thing: YOUR talents and aspirations.

He was highly intelligent but his mind had to be focused or it was all over the place.

His intelligence was wide-angled vision but only gained traction when gently directed by a woman.

I knew it and used my power wisely. I learned never to go to him when pissed off at somebody.

In every case I'd get a sudden insight which would open up new worlds to his great delight.

In every case I interrupted his desultoriness and gave him focus, that's the female intelligence.

## WOMEN GOING BAD

She was filled with the ugly green demon, a total possession of madness, a bad woman.

# TRUST IN TRASH

They told me Pisces had strange antipathies/love hates but I never thought it would be like this.

In every case cuza his love he'd heed my insight and be absorbed for months with God above.

It's not women gone mad but women gone BAD. Use that word, "mad" is what they're proud of.

It's even more disgusting for a woman to be possessed than a man cuz more is expected of them.

It's as though God absorbed up all BAD in your past then He threw  out the entire bag.

## FEMALE DEMONS/REPENTANCE

One can be possessed from mom, dad, siblings, past- times, readings, media: ENTRY POINTS.

We all have sins, all men are sinners, and thus we all have demons to rid through repentance.

God said He forgot it, put it in the deepest part of the ocean/as far as east from west, got it?

Crazy insane things happen with Satan in control, so many it's not necessary to think of the old.

Satan gets us thru self-devaluation until we think we're nothing. Get identity thru accomplishment.

They see the wearing out of parts [getting old] but the sage is more meaningful wholes.

## RECIPE FOR BEDLAM

Recipe for bedlam: You're entranced so you don't dive deep to see the substance of the man.

# TRUST IN TRASH

Will you want style or substance when chips are down and you need his help & no one else around?

Enontiodromia: I was the in a lowly cabin in nowhere now I'm in a lovely mansion with views nuclear!

So I'm just your servant, a bus station for your friends, a place to dump someone to wait, oh yah.

Take the dude in the corner, he loves God and loves you. Tidy him up a bit, nice duds/new shoes.

He will be what you need and love you so much he'll heal all those hurts you've accumulated in life.

So forget the man with style or the gadabout. Look for true substance then let out a shout.

Don't pass over a real man for an imaginary plastic one cuz within a short time they're no fun.

With the right man you won't have to over-analyze. He'll be dependable and protect you guys.

## SUM COST FALLACY

Sum cost fallacy: the more a man invests in you [time, money, energy] the more he will like you.

You don't want a man who's stable/loves you but the one hot and cold triggering those chemicals.

When we come into our reward after years of setbacks one benefit is we can remember no more.

The effects of rejection on the personality: It means to be refused, loathsome, hated and useless.

See the difference between being rejected [could be winning out] and these feelings, false.

# TRUST IN TRASH

Suddenly I just wanted my own stuff--music, art, inventions, thought--and rejected all else.

You can tell she's trotting out sexual magic in new profile pics. Think about it, you don't want this.

Attraction isn't new age, it's affinitization cuz you know people wanna be with people like them.

Never chase a man, just want a relationship and let him compete with the others. for it.

If he's interested of course he's following everything you say and if he isn't to hell with him anyway.

Girls gotta dial it back to zero so his masculine thing can kick in about being the one conquering.

What matured him was knowing I wasn't going to bother him. Alone in his man cage he's in heaven.

## THE CONTAGION OF MADNESS

The spread of hate--the contagion of madness--happens so quickly in human herds I took it as first.

Cancel culture: some people get a pass and some don't. It's like mean girls in junior high or in clubs.

You can't violate the woke liberal orthodoxy or your reputation is murdered and you're crazy.

"I'm uncomfortable" is just a catch-all as you can make anything happen like it's all your domain.

Don't call it attraction, call it affinization: we choose people on the same life level, affinity.

So your body is worth steak and lobster and some drinks? Really? Ha ha what a joke you are lady.

# TRUST IN TRASH

Since I stopped chasing you I feel so much happier, more content, more energy for sure, a seer.

## THE ARCHETYPES

An archetype is not a person but a strata in the brain coagulating through symbols e.g. insane.

Superior man is unique but conformists form archetypes like that of common cartoon characters.

You may have been a good-lookin' kid but now you're in a lower archetype which resembles a pig.

In the estate lawyer's office I felt terror, duplicity, deception, self-dealing and I trust this.

As always happens offspring of the new affluence became vacuous: boastful/prideful/callous.

In the war everything had been taken from them even whole families. There was no ego see.

## THE FIFTIES WERE LOW KEY

To understand personality of the fifties you must know the holocaust but the new kids were lost.

Instead of teaching em what life is really like--the holocaust--they taught em sex/demoralized.

Once they're into sex they're lost for life--no more hobbies, projects, decency, being nice.

They also taught em "man is good"--the biggest lie of the century, basis of virtue signaling/paganism.

So have sex with anything/everything cuz all men are good and brazen women don't lose a thing.

The lack of lines is disgusting--that's what happens when the structure falls out/church is faking.

Pastor got ahold of me and said the most important thing to tell modern women: Never Chase a Man.

Pastor said to us: Never trade your body for a dinner no matter how expensive--get some class.

When the church starts faking it the whole thing goes in reverse and it's dirty demons running it.

Sex does not equal love but the woman always feels that deep down, that's the unequal problem.

Instantly she is unequally yoked and also seen in a negative light even with wicked blokes.

## DUNNING KRUGER AND SEX

Dunning-Kruger effect is overwhelming in small towns when we're understood by NO ONE/not one.

The lowly see life through low archetypes and the one they cast you in was despicable to them.

I was terrified in land of No Understanding. With temps soaring at 120' they were also often angry.

A hot & mean small town was my prison sentence which I overcame by excelling the opposite way.

The second fallacy is that sexual attraction equals love. He likes your shape so you think: I'm it!

Just because a man is excited about you does not mean he's excited about YOU--think this through.

A man with arrested development and a soul like a prepubescent young boy just wants SEX!

Just cuz he's sexually excited about you doesn't mean he even likes you, in fact he could hate you.

Men are such pigs they sleep with women they don't even like. A hole in the wall, anything--yikes!

## REPERCUSSIONS OF BEING CHEAP

She's thinking if she gives him sex she'll be The One. But sexual access does not mean approval doll.

A man will keep having sex with her but NEVER treat her as wife or truly approve of her in that light.

I can't underscore the importance of chastity when seen in this light. Being cheap is a disease, a blight.

## SPIRIT OF DISHONOR

Lesson Two: Your style is cramped cuz you're holding onto people who are dishonoring you.

There are two lives: preparing/overcoming and misery vs. the new life which is wonderful you see.

If I walk into a room and feel the spirit of dishonor, I'm gone. I'm not dealing with that again hon'.

If I've been bad, I repent. But if I live honorably and you're that way I'm just gonna separate.

Why you hanging on to those not interested anymore? People aren't important, they come and go.

People are so fickle a whole town can get against you then disperse and not remember it too.

I had the experience of a whole town against me due to the ruthless gossip of a few in treachery.

# TRUST IN TRASH

I experienced a family against me due to the ruthless calumny of two sisters, opinion leaders.

The whole system can change overnight and they change together. Be very careful of systems sir.

Contagion of madness is Social Psychology. The social comes first, ready to mold the personality.

I had the necessary fire for genius: [OE] over-excitability--if I could overcome reactive hostilities.

Few people individuate. Most are herd animals so don't see them separately but as a whole system.

The superior man individuates into his unique predesigned template but most stay third rate.

Those. who cannot be molded are hated. It's the way social psychology works, we're regulated.

## GOSSIP, CALUMNY AND LITTLE MINDS

Calumny, or the killing of one's reputation--soul murder--is a giant obstacle with few overcomers.

Quit talking about a former spouse or church. They're former for a reason, you're rid of the curse.

It's obvious when a person grows cold/disinterested but you're trying to get em back in the nest.

When they disengage it's disrespectful of the value you bring into the relationship so give them up.

They become disengaged due to hidden offense. Most people if they feel offense never address it.

They'll talk about the offense to everyone else but not to the person with whom they're offended.

This covert empire behind surface reality--a cobweb bind--is too much for a genius mind.

There's an ebb and flow to the gossip grapevine of little minds but a small town is a special grind.

Walk into a room, enter a cobweb of interlocking jealousy systems in the contagion of madness.

I couldn't read it, it was like Greek to me. Ever-changing rules of adaptation to the herd was eerie.

Rather than straighten it out with the offender they turn the hearts of other people against her.

They're disengaged cuz their heart has turned against you but lack the maturity to come to you.

They let that stuff fester while Satan plays with their imagination and soon you got a war going.

If they disengage for any reason you gotta let em go, not continue to get their attention you know.

## LIVE RIGHT/GOD TAKES EM OUT

If you mean right or do right God takes em OUT or brings em IN for your protection or edification.

Prodigal Son left his father who favored him as a prince for friends insulting him eating with pigs.

He saw the difference in the two worlds. Don't enable people to not experience the famine first.

When he came to himself he saw the servants ate better than he. Let people go to wake up quickly.

Sometimes you gotta let a person go 'til they come to themselves. It's not tough love just a hiatus.

# TRUST IN TRASH

Perfect reason: Let em go to find themselves and when they come back they're a different person.

If you can't let em go, ask yourself: Have I deified them? A Jezebel spirit places this hook right in.

## STAY A LEGEND

You're a legend so stay a legend: don't get close to them or a spirit of familiarity makes you a victim.

You wanna turn it all around like I'm dishonoring you when actually it was you dishonoring my home.

It's not about Girls Night Out just re-appraising her Sexual Market Value: seeing if she still has it.

When choosing a mate never ignore you discernment and intuition alerting you with right or wrong.

Never settle on a man who doesn't agree with your spirit. If there's any discordance you will know it.

Never choose a man for identity or purpose. Before you marry please go inside and find yourself.

Only if whole should you engage in/entertain a relationship--or you'll ignore signs to avoid it.

How sad to hang on to relationship from fear of losing identity or purpose. It's a psychotic loss.

God instructs from within our spirit. When he alerts us to right/wrong we hear it/it's death to ignore it.

## NEVER CHASE A MAN, LET HIM WIN YOU

I'm not gonna chase you ever again/anymore. It messed with my head, I'm a woman not a conquerer.

# TRUST IN TRASH

And I'm not gonna compete with a stable of women either, I'm Number One or I never knew you sir.

Losing femininity is not about makeup or dress it's about chasing a man like an aggressive witch.

NEVER chase a man, let him win you. A classical man won't want to be chased by women too.

Only pimps want to be chased, kings want to conquer. Pimps string her out so she's begging for.

Chasing a classical man [husband material] will confuse the synergy of male/female energy.

We live in a world where bad's good, good's bad, women are manly/men are feminine unlike Dad.

A classical man will not be turned on or moved by a woman aggressively pursuing him.

## FEMINIST MAD PURSUIT

The feminist madly pursues anything she wants--it's a sign of our times and a definite turn off.

Classical man ain't in it for the sex and he's easily turned off by her cheap tricks and chasing [hex].

He relents at your aggressive pursuit but later you think he's too timid, a lack--the chemistry's off.

If he gives into her aggressive pursuit later she thinks he's too timid, a lack--the chemistry's off.

A man who gives into her chase will later be weak when called upon to defend, champion, pay.

When she becomes the kind of woman who doesn't need a man she's what a real man needs.

# TRUST IN TRASH

Women: never chase! For when you chase you lose all your feminine appeal--don't compete either.

Let all the other women chase him--to hell with all of em. Just continue the great work with devotion.

Women: What I've said here will save you light years of precious energy. Now you can relax see.

There's something strangely unattractive [eerie] about a woman who's so desperate and chasey.

You think First Lady Trump would ever chase a man? It's inconceivable that she'd ever do that.

Chasing characteristics: Calling too much/more than him, setting up dates or popping up where he is.

Or going public over social media before he said anything or your profile changes to include him.

## WOMAN THE GLORY OF MAN

The woman is the glory of the man. A man wants to WIN a woman so he can be proud of her then.

She's hasn't been around the block/wasn't easy--he had to WORK for her/the others were sleazy.

Being preoccupied with a man who's ill equipped to commit blocks the pull of real relationships.

The dude's been cheating since the beginning but you hang on to the couple status irrespective.

Don't occupy space since it blocks a REAL man coming into your life and a fulfilling relationship.

You have relationship status but you don't have peace, you're unfulfilled and are aging/crying still.

It's better to be alone and fit than to ever choose your couple status over a real relationship.

Mere relationship status doesn't have the right four components: interest/sacrifice/respect/growth.

Most important quip: Is he emotionally available, does he have the capacity for relationship?

Mere couple status is not what God intended but it's what you settled for. Youth should seek more.

Some just want "a man" to go to dinner/take pictures with. How very sad about this generation.

Proclamation to all women: Just cuz he's having sex with you doesn't mean he wants relationship.

Giant insight for most women: In the world of men having sex is just a form of exercise with friends.

## THREE TYPES OF MEN

There's three types of men. The misogynist is driven by toxic masculinity, feeling superior to women.

He's sick thinking he's superior by genitals see. He lacks character, understanding and empathy.

His low emotional intelligence [EQ] prevents him from meaningful partnership with any woman.

I once knew a man with low EQ and he didn't understand me nor tried, he was so focused on "I".

He spent the whole time pumping himself up while being obviously inferior while I was so above.

No, you want a real man ready for relationship to love you, defend the family and manage it greatly.

I don't wanna know beta males/manly women. I like stability while the females are soft-spoken.

Either by training or trauma, the man is a narcissist who won't push his mind to understand you sis.

The pimp is intentionally running games to control you and your mind, he wants you chasing him.

The sad thing is the world conditions women to be attracted to the narcissist bad boy.

Pimp tries to create the brain chemicals and soul ties making you cry out for him in the night.

She wants the man nobody can have. Think of that. The more unavailable the more she's attracted.

Modern Don'ts: She has sex with him but can never have the man so that's the one she wants.

## BEING SINGLE SUX

I was single for years and never wanna be single again. It's like a bull's eye is painted on you friend.

It's well worth it to heed this advice and do it right. Work on yourself not seeking a justifier of "I".

You need protection and want a great home/real life where millions of opportunities alight.

Main problem of the trauma bonded: You give way too much too early but are later confounded.

Then there's the WEAK man with no backbone and easily ruled by a woman. This is called a "simp".

If you settle the pimp will pimp you for life and with the simp you'll never feel safe, it's that simple.

# TRUST IN TRASH

If the weak man is always waiting on you to make decisions how can you ever feel covered?

Is he man enough to lead a household? Kings get queens, simps are disrespected, pimps get old.

Kings conquer queens and kingdoms. They do that cuz they're disciplined/Godly on the bottom.

If you as a queen want a man you can build/grow with you have to wait long enough/not muck it up.

"I been looking for a man" yes but you never left your life available, so occupied with him ya' know.

If involved with a clown too weak to actually lead you or be a man, don't you want a gentleman?

You can't look at a man to see if he's relationship material. People only see sex attraction, that's final.

To know if a man has relationship potential you explore his soul. Questions reveal motives ya' know.

## THE THRILL WILL BE GONE

Lady: "once I stopped chasing the thrill was gone, I took the energy back and didn't really want him."

Queen's questions that only kings can answer. Jezebel is lost, she just seeks to manipulate master.

Simps and pimps are weak and aren't true leaders, they're not deep enough for logical answers.

Kings realize you can't build kingdoms on superficials like the physical. They look into the soul.

Never use sex as dating currency. The world says to want a man you sleep with him--wrong honey.

# TRUST IN TRASH

Sex us not supposed to be used as dating currency for something else like a dam whore dearest.

In my world sex is reserved for a spouse ONLY and about this important thing there is no doubt.

## TRAUMATIZED FEMALE DEVILS

A trauma-bonded and brainwashed female devil: using your body seeking a man's approval.

What does a man offer you equivalent to your body? Dinner? Are you kidding? Oh Lordy...

So you're gonna exchange your God-given body for a dinner? You a low paid harlot, not a winner.

Drinks and steak are equal to your body? Lord women have fallen so low, they sure aren't queenly.

Just cuz he gave you gifts and his company is not enough reason to give your body to a man honey.

Giving sex for anything short of exclusive life-long commitment is degrading/sickening hex.

You're selling dignity for anything you're getting. You know inside you're worth more than din din.

The only proper exchange for your body my sister is marriage. If not marriage material, garbage.

Kings set dates cuz they realize they only have access to queens within the context of marriage.

## REPORTED FOR BEING DIFFERENT

They're trying to demoralize us with homeless everywhere see, and army officers wearing red heals.

# TRUST IN TRASH

In WWII they hated one for being a Jew but now they just hate you without knowing why, it's cool.

Non-Jewish women were put in camps for being different as reported by neighbors and gossip.

I couldn't figure out why she so obviously hated me except I was different with higher IQ see.

Women were expected to act a certain way--script of that era--and they reared up when I spoke ok.

The intelligent unique female becomes the odd girl out bullied by the conformists around--yuk!

Female hatred: I learned to live with it but hated it and increasingly sought solitude until I made it.

If any female is different they'll ask officious questions: "Why didn't you ever have any children?"

It's an insult/self-degrading to even go amongst them unescorted, as I learned forlorned.

Since when is it a measure of character how well you can talk to social phonies? I couldn't you see.

**YOU HURT ME,  I'M DONE SEE**

You hurt me, they hurt me. Don't tell me I'm supposed to suck it up/be friendly anyway, I'm done see.

Face it: you had mental illness at times from malnutrition or what you imbibed--now forget it.

Face it: you were mentally ill before you knew as their persecution made you more heinous too.

\
Their hatred put me in a dark cloud of fear and desperation. It changed my personality son.

# TRUST IN TRASH

Satan took over my life with coping devices to avoid anxiety produced by hatred in society.

The first drink at fifteen felt like a load of bricks off my shoulders, relief at last, my spirit soared.

It was all downhill from there altho' in school I excelled and managed to finish while sinking in swill.

The jealousy in women led them to do awful things, Of women like my sisters I grew terrified see.

Women won't duke it out & get over it like men, they choose lifelong battles especially with kin.

Crutches: alcohol, drugs, food, men. I was a cripple but now am free to be me with real friends.

Changes are scary/speedy: Suddenly a sister was queen bee controlling my husband not just me.

## BALANCE OF POWER

Strife is an enemy sent from hell. it gives you headaches, gut-aches and ruins life like a poison pill.

If no one gets you without a bunch of people too, high-end friends will eventually say POOH!

Suddenly the balance of power changes and like a chess mate you're sunk. It's over/you're bunk.

Her biggest weapon is gossip and calumny: hens going for recognition will ruin your reputation see.

Your number of friends doesn't mark character either. It more likely indicates dunces status/loser.

You think you could have that gang of female "friends" around you if you're against their views?

# TRUST IN TRASH

Female group membership forces you to narrow your interests and censure your views too.

When I was young the older women were really mean. You see this in polygamy: sisters sweet.

"We are science supporters fighting mother earth rapists while flying in private jets." The ruling class

Stop giving your support to parasites, cowards and traitors in pop culture: support the info war.

Must now let go of toxic shame--that which is passed down. Tho' a sinner it's still not your own.

Let go of historical toxic shame and you'll open up to a phantasmagoria, the present moment ok.

Alcohol is a conduit to the devil so be careful bringing that crap through, I've done it too.

## ALL CYCLES HAVE AN END

Persevere [hang on], all creative cycles have an end. It's God's timing and also the link to success.

I'ts time you let this toxic shame go. It's normal for a time but after repentance it's from long ago.

Just cuz she was a mean witch doesn't mean you were wrong, it coulda meant you're different.

It's striking that leading feminists don't care that big boys are competing with little girls isn't it?

Liberal women put Joe Biden in office and now he's sabotaging scholarships for their girls.

Why dieting is dangerous: You should be eating by your intuition not according to someone's plan.

# TRUST IN TRASH

You say you love me but that's just today, this minute--next you're onto someone else you twit.

The people gossiping against you don't even know you but it spreads like wildfire in the daily wire.

Dates bring on gut pain but that's from detoxing the gut in the smallest interstices/only temporary.

## SEX BASED ON PRECEDENT

Women: Never let a man insist on sex cuz you did it before--no evil contract based on precedent.

He got you once so insists you gotta go on with it--**NO YOU DON'T**, stop it at once you twit.

He insists sex is a contract based on precedent and later you have a trauma bond in the rehab center.

Men are screwing a piece of meat but to you it's deepest love just cuz you're there you creep.

Never exchange sex for a dinner. You think you won cuz he's not just coming over for it, you sinner.

You were doing it but you've stopped it and this brought an eruption in the sinful system didn't it.

## TURNING FAMILY MEMBERS AGAINST YOU

The narcissist will go to your family members and turn em against you to punish and keep you isolated.

So self-compassion is our healing. That means to take naps, sun-baths, pet therapy, enjoy music/movies.

When it comes to narcissistic abuse it doesn't matter if the person's dead--it's inscripted in you instead.

He is not above blackmail. These people want only to win and get the job done--whatever it takes hon'.

His mark: He denies, attacks then reverses positions by calling the victim the offender of him, the shark.

The Theory of Blaming Others is disastrous in its effects on young minds because it always means violence.

What they say about the police is pure fabrication easily disproven: blacks are murdered by their own.

The BLM line is that both police and white vigilantes are mass murdering blacks and people believe it.

## NARCISSISTIC SUPPLY

It's all about getting new supply but what if he's hoovering and chatting up old supply? It's all sly.

They need attention all the time--we're talking self-esteem boosts from fans and admirers all in a line.

Classic Hoover: "I miss you" text. Don't get all flustered--remember what it was like then reject it.

It wasn't that he was so strong but that you were so weak. Now healed you'll never think of that creep.

Overnight, Jews were regarded as subhuman--a debasement similar to the Fallen Hero Syndrome.

Survivor said: Even worse than the hunger and pain was the sudden debasement of being subhuman.

I saw the creepy hypocrisy of peeps when I got married and all behavior suddenly changed towards me.

But when you're DOWN: now all their evil comes out from deep DEEP down in the brown, freely.

# TRUST IN TRASH

## SUDDENLY THEY HATE YOU

Suddenly they hated their Jew neighbors when they had been friends. It wasn't just fear, it's humans.

So this was my journey after that snakebite. Don't think about it just know you'll never repeat it.

For it was a pit of poisonous vipers--gone like a vapor--I just didn't know it having been sheltered.

I didn't know what people were like. I was told everyone was nice. But they're FILLED with vice!

Humans in all centuries: disgusting, grabby, clingy, filthy, dirty, conforming, boring, cold, unfaithful.

These gross instincts from the collective unconscious must be tamed and molded or anarchy's emboldened.

He may be nice/you happy for awhile but then you're crazy with jealousy cuz it's just him you see.

Some cultures are gross, some are covered with a veneer of structure/class but sinners nonetheless.

The wicked terrified me. In my distress I called out to my God and He cleared up the entire mess.

## EMOTIONAL CUTOFF DISSOLVES SYMPTOMS

A true emotional cutoff dissolves your symptoms. If still hooked they will persist cuz it's a system.

It is frightening the bad decisions made to get each other's approval--these women need removal.

If you live for their approval you'll die by their rejection. Durianrider
If you live for their approval you'll die by their rejection. You're so much happier never thinking about em.

# TRUST IN TRASH

Musica, good herb, fruit juice and rice. This life in a mansion in the red cliffs is so nice.

I've now returned to my salsero beginnings as a trumpeter under the name Maria Civetta. It's a new era.

And here they said I had multiple personalities and needed to be locked up for it--imagine that.

I can't do it cuz I'm scared. I'd rather create not be afraid. Enjoy my works but just let me disappear dear.

The fact he was rich is what made it so insidious. A Hindu entering our Christian family totally changed us.

I've gone totally into the musical right brain. That means no more words or quips, I'm in retirement.

Straighten this out and you've the solution to wrinkles/age: Is it sugar or FAT which causes ugly glycation?

I think back to the days when musicians entertained us before they started embarrassing us.

Are you really hateful? Or is that just false accusations from your alter ego/critical parent long ago?

## THINKING IS VERBOTEN

They wouldn't let me think, they resented my thoughts. I'd be on a deep plane and they'd small talk.

One time a man yelled at me for thinking when I shoulda been attending to him--it's culture repeating.

I was so lost in my thoughts as a child mom bought a statue of The Thinker and that's me sir.

I was so lost in my thoughts an employer fired me for looking like I was off in a distant sea.

# TRUST IN TRASH

I was so lost in my thoughts it angered me when mom would yell at me to come back to reality.

Not until now, married and behind a gate, can I think all day in peace and not see it as laziness but greatness.

For women are expected to ATTEND to others and thinking is not permitted--some even get a whippin'.

## HE'S JEALOUS OF YOUR THOUGHTS

If we went silent and I went into my head he'd get resentful and jealous I wasn't thinking of him instead.

And if you DO slip into sex don't ever let him tell you it's a CONTRACT--stop the demon hex and relax.

Only now am I protected in order to BE alone. It's the apex of life realizing the value of marriage/home.

I rarely see him but he keeps my head above water and my homelife stable and sustaining--that's it honey.

What does he get out of it? Life in a beautiful home with healthy routines and perfect order, that's all.

I can still hear people yelling at me and I suppose that's how it always will be. We all have a history.

Due to the internet, absurd and extreme concepts like Holocaust denial are now readily available.

There are men averse to any discussion of narcissistic abuse--they say the problem's in YOU.

## MUST GO NO CONTACT

When you finally realize things will never change you go NO CONTACT or Low Detached Contact.

# TRUST IN TRASH

It's about who you let in your life, realizing what's at stake with a lapse in judgement/break in boundaries.

You cannot heal from trauma while also continually being exposed to it: No Contact is the essence.

One of the horrific outcomes of psych abuse is the contamination of our beliefs and worldviews.

Since the goal of the narcissist is to STRIP us of our worth and self-esteem, with the devil he's a team.

What he also takes is our ability to know what is true and not true. What else is mental illness I ask you?

Abuse leaves her so unsure of herself and damaged that even when away from him her life is trashed.

## NON-VERBAL IS IT

After called "worthless" the victim agrees to some degree--it's confirmed by his actions/neglect you see.

He uses NON-verbal ways to get the message to us that we're worthless. He doesn't have to say it miss.

Being held accountable for things we didn't do, being raged at, humiliated and mocked really sux.

After years of being exposed to lack of empathy and told or shown we're worthless, do we not think it of us?

## SELF-COMPASSION IS THE GOAL

The main outcome from abuse so tragic is a mean, cruel, abusive inner critic who is always on our back.

And thus part of the healing is treating ourselves with empathy and compassion. Every day, amen.

# TRUST IN TRASH

To get out of victimhood, first validate you ARE a victim, then empathize for all you've been thru ma'am.

Since we were never shown empathy we don't have it for ourselves or even ask HIM for it, what a laugh.

First step in healing is to empathize and VALIDATE what we've been thru: out with self-doubt Sue.

With commitment to total healing and success you will finally come to self-compassion, your nest.

Narcissists are fiercely protective of their false self and vision--they do it by saying THEY'RE the victim.

Narcissistic rage follows narcissist injury--the biggest of which is you finding out about his  insanity.

## LEVELING

Expect his technique of leveling: something you did is just as bad as his shenanigans and messing.

IF NOT WORSE than what they have done. This is a bait and trap situation you must escape hon'.

If you're an empath with a selfish narcissist there's no way anything you did was equal to his!

It's easy to get empaths to consider maybe he's right--but don't take the bait, that's your only fight.

If none of this works they use the trump card: the smear campaign--ALL associations they contaminate.

His favorite one is saying you're crazy or mentally unstable. You get so mad you think maybe it's true?

He's nothing but the devil. He hurt me bad and I never even met him/love him tho' he's fullabull.

## REPUBLICAN PUSSIES

Conservatives have become pussies. We're afraid to wear a MAGA hat or to speak out lest we're beaten up.

With a lack of good strong male leadership there'd be only pleasing the correct crowd which is Marxist left.

Preachers have failed and become more milquetoast with each generation. They don't preach against sin.

People don't wanna hear about sin so the preacher tailors his sermon around that, diluted powerless crap.

In the congregation lies adultery, homosexuality and thievery but these sinners stay naive and drowning.

Because we had a black president, they don't call us "racist" less they call us "racist" far more, and deplore.

Atheism and socialism is conquering America--growing in leaps and bounds. It's scary, a big black cloud.

Fallen preachers are advancing socialism via social justice sermons and it's severe heresy/non-Christian.

Stop feeling remorse for what you did in dense liberal environments, out of pure fear and confusion.

## BIG BLACK CLOUD OF SILENT HATREDS

The liberal town a big black cloud full of silent hatreds and revenge thru flying monkey coalitions against one.

That same liberal town lets the criminals go free and yet they viciously/mercilessly persecuted thee?

They hated you cuz you wouldn't truckle like they had to. It's all a hierarchy of dominance-submission systems.

# TRUST IN TRASH

If you don't own your home, whoever does can allow others into your home and that is **HELL ON EARTH**, do tell.

Privacy and solitude is **BLISS**, power, excitement, continuous creativity. Loss of privacy = the most utterly shitty.

I didn't have the nerve to say "No, not tonight--I just wanna be alone." No, instead I let him in, and was done.

They wouldn't leave me alone. They were obviously jealous of my privacy or the fact I didn't want frenemies.

You voted for hell, now you're catching hell. She loves the evil around her, it makes her feel powerful.

Peaceful Protests: We're told this is Martial Law by trump in his feeble, lackluster, gelded, soft soap response.

They got the distinct/scary feeling that fanatics, hooligans and eccentrics had secured the upper hand.

The sudden fear that there was a force suddenly--that was so unyielding, so uncaring: that was Nazi Germany.

They introduce sub-standard literature so they can have a black author. It's the same for women: this is awful!

## MICRO-CHEATING

Bad things do not become exempt in small amounts. Greg Gutfeld

Is it micro-cheating or are you becoming paranoid? Is it micro-aggression or some book your read?

MICRO is just that: invisible, you can't see it, you're surmising it because that's the matrix but you INTUIT it.

Overgiving shows weakness--like you're not enough. You want them to like you so give em all your stuff.

# TRUST IN TRASH

Micri-cheating is nonsexual but divides attention from a monogamy setup—the wife  knows it in her solar plexus.

Over-giving: a form of micro-cheating esp. when it's a way of getting attention or making her like the bum.

I see you throwing toys and things at this person to keep them engaged. You can't even see it you fake.

You wanna keep em hooked, keep that connection--and meanwhile they see you as way less-than.

Over-giving is **WRONG**. It's desperate, needy and the receiver will keep you on simmer forever.

They'll keep you on the back burner to be available in the future--it's cruel to yourself and your others.

## PRESENT ONLY YOUR SELF

Present only your **SELF**. Don't form relationships for the wrong reasons or they'll backfire into hell.

If you've been over-giving, dial it back and see if that person is still interested in you. Can you?

If married to an over-giver, take note who he gives to and what your solar plexus [chronic gut ache] tells you.

It's mental adultery thru over-giving to an outsider to get their attention--often with the spouse's agreement.

GIVING: How else could an old coot get a cute chick's attention? It is despicable and not of heaven.

MICRO: It doesn't matter if the receiver is hooked up, he just wants her attention and to make her think of him.

The lady said "it's not that I'm brokenhearted but that I'm shocked, belittled, degraded and disgusted."

# TRUST IN TRASH

When in total confusion [is he a saint or demon?] let your solar plexus tell you hon'--trust your **INTUITION**.

It's not about the person but the contradictions. They are traumatizing, a disappointment, destruction.

Blurred lines: no clear demarcations or monogamy-declarations, he micro-cheats all day hon'

I can't even remember the person--he is not memorable. But the contradiction felt in gut like a deep hole.

I can't turn this thing around. It's gone too far/repeated too much and I'm looking for greener ground.

## THE RECOVERED LADY SAID

You can't rail at someone in a rest home. Eventually you have to go within, deal with it and forgive them.

Falling to that level is so sickening, so untrustworthy, so dark and dirty, so cold and ruthless: we're sick of this.

She got thru it, can't even remember the old coot--but the trauma felt in the gut was so deep in her root.

"I don't wanna discuss it again it's too deep in your root. Now God will deal with you on this while I <u>renew</u>."

STOP railing about him and only ask yourself: How the hell did you ever get involved and how to get out?

They consume so much of our life energy studying about narcissism. Without them life would be heaven.

Of course you're gonna be triggered if you have a history of contradictions and pain from this partner.

Say WOAH buddy, this is feeling very similar to something in the past. We must discuss this.

# TRUST IN TRASH

This feels like that deep dark cavernous betrayal years ago, this is your other side, the one I don't wanna know.

To fight a war isn't it necessary to know the mind of the enemy? I am sure so, it strengthens thee.

**HOOK UP TO GET BACK**

Women cheat cuz they wanna be equal with men and they perceive men as promiscuous by definition.

The ease with which they can "hook up to get back" at some perceived slight makes cheating constant.

**DEPRESSION** lifts when you take your focus off of him and back onto yourself. Instantly you'll feel relief.

The lady says "he pretends to be alpha but can't control his moods--he's definitely beta": she's unmoved.

White refined sugar has **ZERO** glycation--it doesn't age cells. Put it on your grapefruit to increase carbs then sail.

All I know is I have **ZERO** acid reflux and feel incredibly calmly but never have I slept so deeply and completely.

**PROMISCUITY MAKES YOU UGLY**

Incurs jealousy by sleeping around and broadcasting it but it makes him ugly from the spirits inhabiting him.

Here he's doing what he's doing [a whoremonger] yet judging you on the smallest trivial things, a conformer.

People put their best foot forward then come out of their bag as time goes on. Little by little respect is gone.

They use false advertising and dreams to get you in the gate then you see the cracks indicating the third rate.

**LURING AND BAITING**

# TRUST IN TRASH

When he says he has a girlfriend but that it is ending soon like it's no big thing, he is what we call "cushioning".

There's two things: luring someone in, and BAITING them thru provocation and that can be pure sadism.

Baiting is to take you from feeling calm and content to jealous, envious, flustered, triggered, scared.

They want to provoke then gaslight you--its intended to make you lose control. That's different from luring ya' know.

Cushioning, as opposed to micro-cheating, is buying oneself time/moving space tho' they could be the same.

It means he's cushioning you--preparing you--in case he later decides to leave his girlfriend too.

They're modern day pitfalls on relationships as liberalism relaxes previous molds, so get hep and be bold.

They wanna provoke you into meltdown so they can blame you for it--to cover their own naughty behavior.

It's all about getting back at the ex or getting the ex back. That't what happens if you don't let it go: fact.

## AGELESS CORNUCOPIA VS. BULLIES

It's Ageless Cornucopia vs. bullies and sick systems: psychopathic serial bullies in your family.

Bully is shockingly real, about the kids. Unrestrained sex and scapegoatism everywhere/lost their lids.

Violent teen epidemic is rampant--it's anti-authority esp. parents who in fear lock bedroom doors at night.

It stems from two things: (1) taking God out so anything goes, and (2) kids rule and parents are fools.

He fears going solo in the devil's crowd, but the companion of fools and thieves shall be destroyed.

When "protectors" create a bigger void and solitude is avoided it's the soul which is destroyed.

Who is the target of bullies? The gifted, the different, the misfit, the inward and genius/nonconforming.

Mates of she-bullies: Even when things go well they're walking on eggs, fearing the shifts.

Bully keywords: power, control, domination, subjugation, manipulation, intimidation.

## BULLIES ARE ABOUT NARCISSISM

Bullies are about: narcissism, attention seeking, arrogance, isolation and esp. exclusions.

Bully tactics: disempowerment: making impotent, institutionalizing or declaring incompetent.

Bullies take control of finances or perceptions in ritual humiliation and secret alliances against one.

The Lil' Old Lady bullies by stimulating fear and embarrassment by telling all you told her.

In this system, nobody really walks tall. You must separate, see their gall--then you rise as they fall.

All members of bully groups are sick but the identified one is the victim due to her persecution-tantrums.

Violence of bullies is almost entirely psychological, leaving no scars or evidence while they peg you.

With the victim's justified reaction, the Bully pegs it a "mental health problem"

# TRUST IN TRASH

Only a saint could remain calm in the face of blatant cruelty so her justified anger is a "mood disorder".

The frustration from being misjudged leads to her aggression, sickness, addiction or depression.

Her sickness-in-reaction to bully persecution thus confirms the bad identity almost like a confession.

In many cases the victim--rather than self-defending--wards off a fight by simply succumbing.

## BULLIES POWERFUL IN CREATING DESTRUCTION

Bully is powerful in creating destruction so it's you who gets tight but God is your Defender tonight.

These bully studies are so complex you'd have to be a Freud to see why you've been so vexed.

Women manipulate perceptions in a "plausibly and charming" way as you're screwed royally.

Just one's divisive, disordered, dysfunctional personality permeates the system like cancer for generations.

Bully Sue is a practiced liar as power/attention are her gain and when she has the reign, souls are slain.

From bullies you must stay free without refrain for it's your destiny you will again surely gain!

Odd girl out becomes the common target for murder due to the accumulated resentments of the others.

They meet, cheat, plan, justify--to escape boredom. It's much worse than agitation--it's reptilian whoredom.

School phobia from bullies: I didn't wanna go to school! Bad parents make em fight it/uncool.

In making them defend themselves against the bully, their tears turned to solace in beer.

What betrayal--truth and dignity on the shelf. No more kids as happy elves as into hobbies they delve.

To avoid persecution and for protection he makes friends who become possessive/controlling.

Abuse from jealousy of gifts, bringing rifts. Women are most competitive as loyalty degrades (hardly lifts).

The self-hating bully hurts animals (the weak). It's a mean streak and how they all join the clique.

## MUST WATCH TEEN BULLIES

With teen bullies, see the signs and educate the heart--the gentle smart (kindness) you must impart.

Youth abuse pets in spite! Parents: defend the weak (be a knight) when they scapegoat (in delight).

Bullies: interlocking jealousy patterns impute fear, shame and guilt while playing victim.

Emotional bullying is so subtle in the form of a refusal to recognize, value, acknowledge and praise.

Female bullies are masters of manipulation of emotion (guilt and shame) and neediness cues their game.

The elderly, ill or emotional are favorite targets to distract from bully past-times  of being maggots.

BullySue is adept at minimizing/destroying a public image by creating doubts and sharing "concerns".

Poisoned minds is hard to undo so expose the mask and memorize these tactics--an humanitarian task!

She-bullies forge alliances with them as the sole source of info portraying the target as irresponsible.

The victim is pegged "unstable/untrustworthy" from past breaches of trust as bully forms an army.

BullySue gossip is pure projection–the "pot calling the kettle black" and it means ruin/destruction.

## BULLY SUE WANTS DEPENDENCY

Bully Sue wants family's dependency on her for info/lame analyses and anyone blocking is the new target.

To block exposure quickly bullySue feigns victimhood to distract attention as the injured party.

When victim explains the game she is called "paranoid" for seeing, setting and saying things straight.

She bullies are devious, manipulative, cunning, sly, clever and subtle as they "bully with a smile".

Female bullies will often get males to do their dirty work (violence). Have you witnessed this by chance?

## FALLEN HERO SYNDROME

Fallen Hero Syndrome: In purity he shoots to star success, in sin he spirals down just as fast.

Hero begins as pure talent most likely to succeed. He has obvious potential–greatness to rule and lead.

Hero can't act–too weak due to sin: spirit refracted into sensual pastimes that warp, dull, degrade again.

Having refused to stand up/do his duty, Hero falls into hands of an angry jealous mob who tries to kill him.

# TRUST IN TRASH

Sin cannot be predicted: it keeps you longer/costs more than planned and destroys dreams/it's a scam.

It's not just sin bringing him down but also people accelerating his decline in Fallen Hero Syndrome.

## EITHER LEAD (GAIN RESPECT) OR BE SLAIN

Either the Hero leads and gains respect or loses and brings their impulses to slay--that's a fact.

Mob jealousy inevitably explodes against great-going-down: "who did he think he was trying to rule US?"

Once his down-spiral begins nothing changes its route. The consequences of sin are inherent in sin itself!

Simply put, sin contains its own punishment. It's inherent in sin itself, God doesn't need to do it.

Hero's getting weaker and is shocked at his sudden decline, then the others chime in to seal his demise.

Like chickens, once one is pecked they gang up to his death. Man acts first then justifies with frontal cortex.

Scapegoat systems surrounding alcoholism: It's very hard to get up once you've been down.

Only true champions--overcomers--can pull themselves back up through repentance, the only answer.

Once our hero is back up he/she must resist temptations and undertow to fall back to the status quo.

Repent ye, then act like nothing ever happened, for it didn't: Sins erased, no longer habit-encased.

It was only habit that made it real. When over, it never was: Hero stays down from cycles of sin/systems.

# TRUST IN TRASH

## UNIQUE SEED POTENTIALS BLOSSOM WITH REPENTANCE

Born as unique seed potentials of peculiar talents (true genius), a blueprint-destiny is expression of God.

True genius is terse, laconic and wise.

As easy as a bird singing, finding our groove is world success--a dormant potential until repentance.

As such very few geniuses are developed cuz in this generation they don't even realize they should repent.

Never trust revelation unless pure, or suffer "autonomisms"--twisted/stupid uprushes from unconscious.

True genius is from God--the dark soul remains the bad act, would-be genius, has-been-who-never-was.

Einstein: it's all just energy. Thus "sin" is recycled energy in outworn channels--pure useless repetition.

## DEMOCRATS ARE GLOBALISTS

Democrats aren't Americans, they're globalists. They've signed on with the Chicoms, the EU and apple.

Quick-to-shoot carnal drives block energy and the serpent recoils tighter each time one gives in, see?

Each time it's easier for the bad memory to trigger craving to sin and we lose public/private power.

With repentance, a spiraling release of energy up the spine: saved from the misery of the sin-filled life.

The reward of repentance: unleashed forces--the blueprint potential at birth. Now just do your work.

With repentance we have a psychic opening: like splintering glass pure light shatters darkness of sin.

# TRUST IN TRASH

Oh happy days--one wonders why he waited so long to give up these useless burdens/now you hate sin.

The rush of released energy unleashes True Genius: With conversion the saints were overnight successes.

Having fruitlessly striven for decades their work blossomed as angels brought the Great Work to completion.

## REPENTANCE:  BEING CARRIED DOWNSTREAM

Repentance: It's as if the ex-sinner-now-saint's being carried downstream in spite of himself, what a lift!

The repentant know the worst sinners are the most grateful saints, for they have joy and no more restraints!

To sin is to miss the mark--the blueprint destiny at birth/true success--and life is boring, painful, stark.

God wants our expression as designed before conception. What blocks this? Blindness is the problem.

In times of mass sin/chaos prophets rise to tell sinful masses what is hidden by sin but should be obvious.

Because bondage is a bandage the wise and wealthy become fools "despicable, naked and blind."

Because humans can learn to tolerate anything, prevalent sin is taken-for-granted as "normal."

It is only rare strength--true nobility--that is independent from the masses and can take a moral stand.

"Wide is the path to destruction but narrow is gate to eternal life." Sinful man is weak/caves in to strife.

The liberals think this present moral breakdown has always been around--it's just "out of the closet" now.

# TRUST IN TRASH

Not the same: human race goes through cycles of moral degeneration and regeneration--ups and downs.

Moral downs precede barbaric invasion--often from within, bringing on movements of revitalization.

In the "ups" monogamy reigns, families stay together, creative people prosper, low addiction/self-discipline.

UPS: order and simplicity--truth prevails. DOWNS: families disperse, addictions are epidemic, prosperity dies.

## TRASH IS CHAOTIC CLUTTER

During the down phases there is trash: chaotic clutter (morbid accumulation) prevails/decency is bashed.

Through gradual desensitization sin is tolerated (taken-for-granted-as-normal) and culture is obliterated.

Sin's a collective dark force and social hypnotism like the dirty debauchery in 19th century England.

Every generation has it's favorite sins which are fashionable, then prophets tell the blindly disabled.

Truth hurts (people love their sins) and prophets are stoned ("they will hate you as they hated Me")/alone.

Saints sense over-complexity/superfluity in carnal men but austere simplicity is the truth to genius, amen.

The sinner is forever vacillating, covering tracks, putting on a façade, dealing with guilt and remorse.

The sinner justifies actions, plans how to get more, accumules to compensate and blames others.

Sinner's life is filled with compensations for sin but outer adornment is ill-dignified/for the trash bin.

# TRUST IN TRASH

Sinner fills house with non-essentials and useless complexity like a dime-store or tobacco road, very silly.

Chaotic lifestyle of sinners is intolerable to saint-genius who wants the important to illuminate: winner!

To get to God's power have prayerful life--solitude/space--leaving time for concentration on the highest.

## ARISTOCRATIC NEATNESS

Neatness is aristocratic. Imagine a monastery of austere simplicity, clean feeling of space and total order.

Make your home a reflection of heaven--orderly clean simplicity--not hell: dirty disorder and clutter.

Truth of simplicity clears mind, releasing exhilaration of real energy. Sinful can't de-clutter due to anxiety.

It's a lonely life of loving ancestors who've passed and for the living relatives, disgust.

The sinful man is two people in one. Like alcoholics, all habits create Jekyll-and-Hyde temperaments.

Two nervous systems: one opens up (in love) and one shuts down (in fear) then perception gets queer.

When in sin, no spiritual thoughts only dark clouds. No feelings of love just reasons to hate now.

Is their wrath amongst you? Sin creates the fight-flight mechanism and a jungle mentality view.

Money and success keeps the sinner from repentance/God's rewards so pray the foe gets more!

Animals are such a refreshing breeze from human sleaze.

Wild vacillations of mind--sudden "flip-flops"--indicate sin.

# TRUST IN TRASH

When in sin one feels the "cold shun" from everyone he meets. Does this explain SJWs, ya think?

Conflict creates pressure between who he is and who he says he is, creating sting-shots on those closest.

Internal conflict of sinners are temporarily resolved by exploding on others.

## THE BLIND DON'T FEEL SLIGHTS

Sting shots occur constantly but may be missed by others due to low self-esteem creating blindness.

Sin shows—in appearance, denseness, mistakes, broken relations and missed opportunities.

Concentric circles around sin: Red hot "issues" are created in family and friends as it spreads.

Respect is innate for True Leaders of Men. Dignity is purity and clear vision--a hard moral stand yet loving.

People "clear" around warm steel then the family system. In reverse, contagion of madness from sin.

Dark vacillations are irritating and often dangerous though covered over by apologies and compensations.

Habits are pure repetition and for all animals the mal-adaptation to hostile environments is exhaustion.

Habits: instability and fatigue as swinging moods add to the complexity of sinful life and adapting thereto.

Sinners are at a low vibration of reality in tunnel-vision. True reality is of God, cornucopia/miracle continuation.

Repent: From sin to synchronicity, now everything fits in divine moments filled with cues, signs, symbols.

# TRUST IN TRASH

We should watch for miracles like a cat watches a mousehole. Each moment is a divine design of potential.

To sin is to warp the future, seeding for bad- but in purity we are powerfully unique, universal, recognized by all.

One saint: "I rode on a wave of ecstasy and wondered why I waited so long to give up this useless burden".

From dense to clear: Born clear (unique) we're smashed by the world--tamed to conform our spirit is broken.

## SICK ATTACHMENTS-THRU-DENIAL

Attachments-thru-denial: Are you tamed to conform to the outright lies of those in control over you?

How to be happy and rid of strife: Repent, break free of denial and enter a brand new life.

Break free of denial by recognizing good vs. bad leaders--i.e. between the clear and the cluttered.

Clarity: High self-esteem, creativity, unique unfolding, receptivity, love bringing joy, pure perception.

Clarity: Growth, clear unbiased perception, spontaneity, cannot be controlled, aware of relationships.

Clutter: Low self-esteem, blocked energy, control, regression, fear bringing hate and tunnel-vision.

Dense: Past/future roadmaps and fears, repetition of mistakes, seeing through projections, social hypnotism.

## CRUELIANS

Dense: Hypnotized by relationships.  The sinner is a double-minded man, unstable in all his ways.

# TRUST IN TRASH

Many forsake the saint/genius, loving the present world. Can you still trust God, rejected by boys and girls?

The reward for repentance is right-brain living--a magical, charmed life: synchronicity/no strife.

That's the trick: Though family and friends detest, to pass the test and be the best in whom all now invest.

Creative genius comes out in work you love. You'll be aghast at scary human dramas thick as mud.

## CAREFUL WHO YOU ASSOCIATE WITH

Careful who you put your faith in--who you associate with--since the influence is there with mere contact.

The shark knows this: his sequence is contact, influence, **CONQUEST**.

Conquest is over your mind which ceases to be a lovely garden/starry night and starts being a scene from hell.

When to bad influences you caved you made wrong decisions which degraded your life for decades.

Dissociating from lower elements is the name of the game--separate to re-connect to power and fame.

Popularity means nothing--or do you think just cuz they're accepted you should put your faith in them?

Falling into the popular groove they're out of grace and will only misadvise you on what you should do.

Tragedies from bad influences: scary to realize this but incredibly beneficial to open to beautiful future!

Thinking most people are "nice" is very stupid--stay alert to subtle influences tearing you down, stricken.

# TRUST IN TRASH

Misplaced faith inspires fear which is instinct warning of possible destruction-
-powerlessness felt in stomach.

Faith in an unstable man is like living on quicksand. From highest highs to devastating lows, oh man.

Dulling instincts to avoid recognition of creeps: are you stuffing/drinking down fears on a road so steep?

Become aware of/question associates. You're blocked and you need silence to succeed not games/noise.

Their loyalty is divided between God and the world, and they are unstable in everything they do. James 1: 8

## KEEP CHATTERERS AT BAY

Keep chatterers (using you for entertainment) at bay for these are energy thieves and time is late.

Sins are coping devices to adapt to people in your environment. Man is an adaptive animal/you're mal-adaptive.

Exhaustion is the result of oppression--from letting inferiors worm their way in.

Since hostile environments are sterile dynasties/petty competition, they contaminate/restrict creation.

Dense environments are based on rules you want no part of. Your destiny is genius without map or plan.

Study the ways to escape cruel people then life comes together as hypnotic spells of all systems dissolve.

Now you see the mixed signals keeping you down rather than the blame and shame from their game.

Study the subtleties of human cruelties so you can shake loose from the denial of bad faith tragedies.

# TRUST IN TRASH

Detachment from fruitless relationships brings explosion into new wonderlands--detach then open up, man!

One's Self has been defined against these grounds so detach so that God brings these traitors down.

The wonderful release from people is ineffable as the past's heartbreak dissolves to joy/self-control.

## DETACH: NOW *GOD* DEFINES YOU

Detach so now the universe and God--the lovely moment--defines you. The joyous release is ineffable!

As long as you keep thinking about past creeps they're still defining you and you sink in your swill and stew.

Cruelty is too subtle, silent and insidious to see and thus we only hear of love/goodness, masks of the unfree.

Cruelty is rarely mentioned since as a sinister force it prevents its own exposure and we're less for it.

Learning about subtle cruelty liberates you with perfect protection so learn them for it happens fast, man.

I recall the pains: broken promises/plans, being stood up/kept waiting, gossip-called-concern, a hostile stare.

Cruelty: perverse triangles/secret alliances, sarcasm, dangerous advice or casual misjudgments.

There is active cruelty then passively witnessing or allowing it to occur--in both it's an invisible empire.

Cruelty registers deep, resulting in addictions to avoid anxiety as a pervasive anger takes over.

Denial keeps us hooked to the cruel effects while awareness though painful gives protection/prevention.

# TRUST IN TRASH

Cruelty doesn't leave by ignoring it for like cancer it grows more menacing under the surface, believe it.

See the light to avoid a fight. It's ignorance of cruelty that maintains it and awareness makes it right.

It is good to see the wild wickedness of people for then our great work blossoms and we reap, filled.

Cruelty is subtle so catch it before it clips you. Become as skilled as identifying stars and always see truth.

You must think: "she said that to get revenge" or "he did that to make me jealous cuz he can't control me."

## SEE IT THEN RELEASE IT

No need to confront cruelty--just seeing it stamps out denial/anger. You're now free as the lone ranger.

Despite "loving" image this generation isn't nice as we witness pure hypocrisy and the cruelian is hurt mostly.

The cruelian's first victim is himself since he hates truth and decency as different from him--really creepy.

Some people love getting you into trouble. Stay clear for a chief cause of sorrow is blindness to evil.

The worst part is the blind insisting they can see. Who does this remind you of, the liberals ya' think?

The unhappy climate with a cruelian is marked by frequent fickleness/explosions of suppressed anger.

Had you just known! Learn from that to avoid annoying involvements to which your center says "NO.".

Notice how quickly people change their minds: friendly and helpful then cold, evasive and unkind.

# TRUST IN TRASH

Are your protectors your worst enemies? Don't be dismayed--sad realizations mark growth into maturity.

Let the tears flow then open to the future and oceans of power. You've always known but denial dulls/sours.

Face human haze to get high prize of those set apart from the maize--the misjudgments of masked identities.

## NO FRIENDS = SUCCESS

No friends = success if through bad advice they create a mess.

Dare to see through weakness posing as strength for staying in delusion is heartbreaking for the saints.

Growing up is giving up foolish fantasies about inefficient diets, phony friends and fallacious family fakes.

The more familiar the pain caused by persecutors the deeper the knife—perhaps for your whole life.

You're so used to it you can't think straight anymore! A release about to occur--no more sucker for mockers.

To be champ, delete fools/choose your folks. You must never rely on immature souls pulling the rug out.

As you learn to stand alone you will surely feel much safer with just truth and God as your teacher.

A cruel act is an explosion of suppressed energy. The pressure accumulates from foes smelling like a rose.

An inwardly wrong person is under the pressure of this conflict which regularly erupts causing pain/damage.

When truth finally takes inner hold, cruelians lose pressure from pretense and thus cruelty also goes.

The phony ain't fine so you gotta draw that line. He is gross and un-free: it's his envy you must flee.

The greater your role shall be, the better you'll feel as just "me". People are just an encumbrance, see?

Law of affinity says things of like tone vibrate together. Attractions or repulsions based on behavior.

Wrongness hates rightness so the two can never relate--they walk different paths of love vs. hate.

It helps to know the faker of right is always wrong.

## GETTING HURT BY WRONG PEOPLE

Getting hurt by wrong people reflects denied wrong in ourselves attracted to weakness posing as strength.

The phony is blindly attracted to phoniness. They deserve each other so let em go and find godliness.

Be internally right to receive the safety of that rightness by avoiding the toxic system, your highness!

See it for God's sake--for a romance or friendship with a cruelian is like living with a rattlesnake!

See the truth as a guide in all male-female relations then everything becomes smooth and pleasant.

No wrong man can hurt a right woman by instinct alone/no wrong woman deceives a righteous man who knows.

Lord turned captivity of Job when he prayed for his friends so let's pray: "please Lord help these phonies."

Most common fear is their anger. Knowing the nutty nasty nature of humans deletes fear/leads you higher.

# TRUST IN TRASH

Prince will no longer tremble before rabble. Only the weak wear wrath, yet you weep? No more, you're able.

Declare independence, stay safe and human storms will be of non-effect save resentments from the past.

If you can understand, you command. By giving up delusions your inner journey expands into God's plan.

## DETACH FROM OUTER, IMPLODE TO INNER

Detach from the outer, implode to the inner just by skipping dinner and avoiding the controlling sinner.

Never knew I was mimicking mom the shrew. My apologies to Chuck, Danny, Dwight, Richard, Jimmy and Ray too.

Declare independence, stay safe and human storms will be of non-effect save resentments I'd expect.

What built this country was not rolling over but attacking the enemy.

Cruelians love the thrill of hurting others. Playing games and repeating templates confirms his greatness.

Just when you're happy he falls into his bag: keeping you waiting, forcing you into hardship/irritation.

We've all been attacked: he's making you jealous/feel less, old, unholy, a phony and you buy that crap.

He digs driving you to desperation and that's the power you give him--so just by learning, you win.

Dare to disappoint demanders--never give what you don't want to give. Beware of expectations: abusive.

Discern the valuable from the worthless--egotistical cruelians have no value to you my dearest.

# TRUST IN TRASH

Becoming alert to the harmful or unpleasant builds instincts of the mind as well as boundaries and habit.

No more denial, now you're alert: a rich squirt free of hurts and neurotic quirks cuz you didn't come first.

The cruelian thinks for you--like Elmer Fudd. Refuse the charlatan's two cents and think as you should.

Involvement with wrong can distract/delete decades from God's plan so take control with perfect protection.

"What are you really like behind the mask?" Since he knows he's false he'll either flee or attack.

## THE NICE LADY IS REALLY A SCORPION

See that nice lady? She's really a scorpion. Fakery is the cause of cruelty so escape hurt be seeing the shady.

Cruelians are conquistadors--compelled to win the debate, score the ego point, be a hero--so shut the door!

Instead of deflation think: "this could have been handled in a higher way." So why settle for the lower, ok?

The conquering fool is low lured by like-lowness. He can never see the higher world, not knowing himself.

He wants his wicked ways to work in sin and hates you for your foolish flattery of a fake like him, a no-win.

The fool tries to please the cruelian thinking he'll be loved but becomes weak declaring cruelty is a dove.

Why reward the ruinous, the recalcitrant, the rank? The creepy cruelian can only bring you down: no thanks.

Some fear rejecting misery-makers thinking they need these stinkers. Detach to be true clear thinkers!

# TRUST IN TRASH

It's your awareness alone subduing haters but your blind denial is the glue of gossiping collaborators.

For the cure take a one month bipolar (IN-OUT) diet to weed your friendships who are lying about it.

People are either IN or OUT. The INs you love, adore, cherish and reward, the OUTs you avoid, reject, ignore.

The outs can't hurt you again once you become the master for it was you sending invitations for disaster.

Practice IN and OUT for more relief than you've ever known. No more slights for the King knows the foe.

## HOLD YOUR HEAD UP HIGH

Keep your head above the cruel crowd through aristocratic reserve. Be terse, laconic, sober--observe.

The down-and-outs hate you for placating, pandering to and pleading with their sick, silly and sadistic souls.

Cruelians only love those seeing through them so designate him OUT to bring respect precursory to love.

Make people win your favor by growing up, while never trying to win their favor again just the Lord above.

Your new matrix of IN-OUT is a new future for the relief from tension opens the floodgates energy for sure.

Since all misjudgment is oppressive the IN-OUT matrix removes the block keeping you from success.

Sweet silence says it all--they know what they did anyway so there is nothing to say, just stand tall.

Your golden silence is a siren suggesting they spurt up speedily or "so long, so-low, I'm going solo."

# TRUST IN TRASH

Bringing up the bad past--labels and fables--is a sign of manipulation since Jesus said it is over.

Cruelians love bringing up your (bad) past. Think "ABM": Attack Bad Memories of events that are passed.

Cruelians seek to weaken/confuse you to inflate self but you aren't that person, the true self is reinventin'.

Call a rattlesnake a "kitten" and it's still what it is. Ignore self-flattering labels and just see realities.

Liberals, democrats and dam rats call themselves "loving" to veil viciously vindictive minds.

It's the "humanitarian" groups hogging/hoarding power/wealth so question the popular you love so much.

## CRUELIANS EXCUSE BRUTALITY

Cruelians always excuse brutality—they've a right to attack, betray a promise or rub your nose in the past.

When he justifies, he lies. Worse, his cronies support hypocrisy while his victims call him charming.

To detach, live in your own secret world. We can't change em but can detach thru our journey inward.

Solitude is the mistress to turn to when people problems persist then enjoy the ecstasy of living highest.

Never let em know how childish/ignorant they are. Keep wisdom in your secret world then become a star.

Living in desert solitude I turn turn from man, mass or mess to face the beautiful mountain vistas in bliss.

In the miraculous moment all goes "strangely dim." Everyone's on probation with me cuz I see only eternity.

# TRUST IN TRASH

Phony friends/fickle family contaminated your aura so rise outa reach through regality: just God and thee.

Turn to eternity when all people problems have passed. Think, dream, plan for the future glories so vast!

The cruelian is a pouncer looking for an excuse to scream, attack and injure--his cold eyes make you unsure.

Pain of persecution dissolves when you see the incredible pressure between the true self and the facade.

## THEY EXPLODE WITH POLITE CRUELTIES

They explode with "polite" cruelties as a bio-device to release blocked energy--don't fear, just get insight.

Perception prevents pain while denial allows cruelians to confuse, cajole and cause you to cringe.

The weak talk too much/can't understand why you'd rather think than talk. Let them go the dumb rocks.

Even if you have to live with animals alone, at least you'll get your work done.

After separating it will be effortless. See the divine design then it's a case of beauty from ashes.

The devil's crowd is politically correct. They tow the line saying whatever's popular but not the Elect.

The weak talk constantly, habitually and idly. The biggest drain on genius and reason for boredom, surely.

The weak are so dependent on you they'll come without calling first,  Draw a line for privacy or be cursed.

You must manage people now.  Your work is deep and intricate, they must shut their mouths or GET OUT.

# TRUST IN TRASH

Tyranny of the group wants you down and hopeless making you prove yourself creating more embarrassment.

Say "I can't deal with your projections nor talk again." Overcome subtle yet pervasive obstacles: use assertion.

The dominator adapted to your docility so be assertive baby then new attractions = success, truly.

Just BE right so no more memories, habits or systems take hold. Be like all saints in history: BOLD.

Gossip can't hurt you--it's just a name/label. You've grown weary so declare independence then bye, Mabel.

## DETACH, THERE'S NOTHING THEY CAN DO

When you're out of the system there's nothing they can do so keep saying when down: case closed, whew!

You've been infected but now you'll be better, then best--release this system and transcend to your crest.

If upon waking to the abuse you find yourself without friends, great--you'll now be with God, the highest.

God knows your great future--this present situation is part of your training: unforgettable/heartbreaking.

As you come to your talents remember this: jealousy is their incentive: Make you small/not get so big.

Choice: Faith in wrong people (bad faith) or experience true fullness, for bad faith makes you depressed.

There's no happiness with bad faith as the contradictions are a cancer to the subconscious, ok?

When the tension of denial is gone you're back in the Kingdom: your center, your home.

# TRUST IN TRASH

Acceptance reached brings reversal: you're now in a joyful light so be assertive with many rehearsals.

These people putting painful projections on you care nothing for your joy.

We have a choice: Bad faith or true fullness. Bad faith brings depression while the truth creates happiness.

Bad faith in useless people through denial results in dulled eyes/dense brain and dimmed experience.

## THEY BLOCKED YOUR FASCINATION

With them around to stay you have flagged interest in destiny and projects-- you don't cherish the day.

Everything forced unconscious makes us dense, as our projects dim anytime we deny the obvious.

Bad relationships degrade reality--the hard-won bud of genius. This beautiful seed is smashed by this.

Once the light goes out due to carnal/vulgar or indifferent your creativity is ruined by these children.

When they hear less than 90% get asylum they'll be incentivized to crash the border/more following.

True pleasure is blocked by tension so release prideful people/pastimes and find fullness: ecstasy in life.

True pleasure is blocked by tension, so release prideful people/pastimes and find fullness, a mansion.

## HOME CENTER:  SOLITUDE

We lose identity when enmeshed in groups, mal-adapting by dropping parts of self then being duped.

We should be moving to a more independent reality, not a more enmeshed one then getting silly.

Independence is the discoverer who splits from the majority view which everyone knows is "true".

High boundaries is an essential achievement for success to occur--separation precedes success for sure.

An anorexic undifferentiated early from the family system compensates by going opposite later--total reclusion.

In solitude she learns petty competition/jealousies are instantly dissolved with her total inaccessibility.

## A BLANK SLATE FOR OTHER'S PROJECTIONS

Tho' she was a "blank slate" for others projections she's now warm steel--impervious, cordial but firm.

The female overcomer jealously guards who's around for it is "contact, influence, conquest."

Children love non-competitive games the most: it is independence that brings genius expression/BOSS.

Happiest cultures are non-competitive and genius competes with no one--for in his unique stream there is none.

Competitive groups ruin genius thus rare talent secludes, never compares with others, keeps to himself.

Your essence is your private castle for nothing else compares. Home-centered is SELF-centered, rare.

If your home doesn't reflect you, you lack center and are owned by society. And the dirt and clutter, oh my.

Uncentered: home is in shambles while they travel with the rabble.

Regain center to feel the wonderful joy of knowing the YOU as distinguished from the masses/whew.

# TRUST IN TRASH

Selfishness/domination is described as tolerance/liberation and degeneracy is described as "freedom".

Conspiring to open our borders to foreign invasion--THAT is the biggest charge to Obama of treason.

The non-competitive atmosphere of your home transcends time and space so become inaccessible, please!

## STAY HOME AND CHOOSE YOUR EXPERIENCE

Stay home, choose your experience, make your home reflect your personality and never adapt again!

Choose ALL as you simultaneously seclude. Love your little niche, fill time with solitary pursuits and get rich.

Through the inner journey you gain discernment and high boundaries defining True Royalty, finally.

The opposite of royalty is being emotionally dependent on a vacillator who breaks your heart!

It's the science of silence vs. codependence with a lush or louse.

If one is right then silence is the most perfect way to deal with resistance.

Until one's time has come, fighting resistance only tore him down but surety, silence and seclusion won.

In groups loyalty/protection transcends autonomy/self-realization so they always side against the great ones.

Groups: Denial of self combined with mutual consideration are more esteemed than expression of Self.

For genius there is sanctity to separation and seclusion until his time has come to catalyze the nation.

Be a genius in your field (release into cosmic freedom) or endure the horrors of codependency, dumbed.

# TRUST IN TRASH

Here the dominant one maintains superiority by "advising" then getting angry with independent striving.

Anger inspires fear leading to bad faith/lost fullness. With growth the dominant lay traps but then fall into it.

Put your faith where it belongs: in your own stream and instincts for then God protects your moments.

"Holy" means separate, like God--to be holy is to be separate. Because God is separate, holy is non-ordinary.

## SEPARATE/INSULATE TO REFLECT GOD

Highest religious experience is reflecting divine, so separate/insulate so God shines thru talents refined.

Finish work then rest. A period of "ecstatic rest" is your last phase and for new royalty, rest precedes rule, ok?

I apologize to every male I knew since 14. I was in denial while mimicking my mother who was angry, see?

My military husband wouldn't take it so laid the law down. I got my ears back suddenly, I was in love.

It's a CLICK in the head when you fall into line. No more whine/the arrogance of ego both yours and mine.

Deceivers cause confusion from his anxious face, resentful words and empty life--Lord, I need space!

He puts you in fear as his defeats are your worries. Let this be your blessing for visions spring from crises.

Use the cruelian's terrible traumas and tantrums to reveal solutions while giving you the will to act on them.

God doesn't want you destroyed by evil--only seeing through people brings joy, no more feeble but gleeful!

# TRUST IN TRASH

Ask: "do I want to be here with him/them? Success comes with seeing through the world's false front/"fun".

They do wrong cuz they don't know right so always remember the higher conquers the lower.

Unconsciously they act superior assuming the pecking order is right and you are wrong—social hypnotism.

Don't struggle to win, let God come down on him. It's society vs. God who is on your side and friend.

## CRUELIANS HAVE NO COMPASSION

Never expect compassion from a cruelian unless it's part of his game, remembering he'll change.

Stand in high silence so high science can make his effect null and void. Don't engage and even avoid.

Test the cruelian's terror from being ignored and watch as the hurtful hero cries like a baby's tantrum.

Your denial of what he's really like means one thing: the sly sadist succeeds in leading you to strife and sadness.

Has this not occurred all through your past? You deny, you cry. You buy that lie, then to self-esteem: bye-bye.

Superior insight: Don't fear labels for now you can read people in a new way no matter what their image.

The hard-hearted are miserable, the cruel are lost and the touchy have only pretensions of happiness.

The vicious or vile masochistically prefer self-destructive attacks over a peaceful existence. Vernon Howard

Self-destruction is a painful thrill and the harder they fall (e.g. in love) the quicker they'll turn on you.

When trust is lost, it is lost. Some sneaks are snakes, striking then slithering away for good then you're boss.

Superior insight is the ability to see the reversals and ferocious flip-flops of people: friendly then evil.

OP-TRUTH: all men are two (opposite) people in one as there are two brains and separate nervous systems.

The private and social sides are worlds apart. To deny it you comparmentalize it then soon there is disaster.

For stability in hostile environments think: "it's a package deal" then as Jekyll becomes Hyde, decide.

You get their help but soon you'll yelp. Calmly take note then take a new boat.

If you don't know cruelians this may seem negative. But even you will feel people pain or witness it.

**WELCOME TO A PEACEFUL VIEW**

Now you've a peaceful view. With a new mind you see the connection between fear and behavior towards you.

Anxiety attracts hurt you believe the harsh can inflict but understanding breaks the power of the witch.

Brutal man cries he's changed his ways, appeases with apologies then strikes again. His cries are lies/no friend.

Though a snake learns to kiss he's still a snake. Catch cunning cruelty by asking: is it ego or truth?

Since truth doesn't deceive you know conceit caused the cruelty and exposure makes it powerless, so believe.

Cruel gang demands you plan for their benefit so casually ignore and plan your own right life without em.

# TRUST IN TRASH

Stay free of psychic violence as an anger-detective: sudden silence, sly sarcasm, sullen stares, silly submission.

Anger signs: forced jocularity and coldly polite accusations--now detach from bad memories or emotions.

Whether it comes from sugar or shitty history, strife is a killer: a demon sent from hell to ruin destiny.

Strife is malice, envy, jealousy, anger, resentment and bitterness. It comes thru sin--of act or association.

## SPIRITUAL GIFTS GONE WITH THE RIFTS

Strife means lost meaning and anointing (presence of God) and spiritual gifts are gone with the rifts.

Remember: The cruelian wants to involve us in strife so we must do everything but go to war if we have to.

Stress-based diseases from strife: to the nervous system, organs, and tissues it's like a knife.

Resentments cause disease from asthma to warts. Know why then disease departs.

Cruelian is conflicted, you were the closest victim, period. Wisdom is your shield but denial = no power to wield.

For attention bullies behave brutally to be fearfully noticed with screams or arguments so don't do it.

## HEALTH UPDATES

Fruit makes me energetic and happy all day, everything else hurts and there is hell to pay.

If you don't have good digestion life is hell. The gut aches, the bloat, the praying for death.

# TRUST IN TRASH

People are so entrenched in sugar phobia. They wanna eat fat so they'll eat that if it's ok with ya.

You break an ankle or knee and it's a bummer. It makes you think: will I be around much longer?

Characteristics of a surefire star: They can learn to live on a Cliff Bar and some juice later.

It was a mental illness--whatcha call a fatal one--but with relatives it takes forever to live it down.

There's nothing more frightening then waking up choking & suffocating cuz you ate dinner honey.

Strapless or spaghetti strap for party or home, high neck for news anchors or doesn't seem apropos.

No grains, no fats, no processed. Fruit smoothies are the most painless and once a week some fish.

Handiest fast food ever: dates at your desk. The office frig is filled with juices in addition to this.

The sweets you're eating are filled with fat and that's why you're fat not from the sugar you twit.

## STAY SWEET, KEEP SWEET

Stay sweet, KEEP sweet. Eat fruit and sugar and do your work with great devotion and be patient.

Chanel's hats were elegant and free of fussy embellishments. Austere simplicity is genius.

Is it that the sun causes wrinkles/skin damage, or does it damage already bad skin from food garbage?

"I love doing the cooking BUT I destroy the kitchen". That's a big BUT though, good riddance.

# TRUST IN TRASH

He fixed the greatest Christmas dinners but it took me 3 days to completely clean the kitchen.

Intuitively I know fatty acids bring on acid reflux building ugly tissue of the false body: fat sux.

## INTUITION SAYS FRUIT IS SAFE

Intuitively I know fruit makes me sweet/cute/childlike while everything else evokes immune spike.

No more garlic, onion, caramelization, raw salads, grains or anything else poking holes in the gut.

Good digestion equals happy life. Bad digestion means days of excruciating pain, torment, cries.

No more tomato sauces simmering all day for the delicious taste. It's holes in the gut, ok?

Tho' it seems rice noodles will be soft enough, it's still grains. and you still get holes in the gut.

Caramelization is the most delicious cooking son but brings the greatest aging: GLYCATION.

A choker: macaroni and cheese for dinner. Grains mixed with animal fat, later you're gasping for air.

## FROM FAT TO STARCH REVERSALS

Sometimes only watermelon quenches not water, cuza that I could never go lowcarb either.

I was used to soft foods like grapefruit and avocado so then grains like rice/corn poked holes in my middle.

I need baby food not "fiber" feeling like nails in my gut. Read Fiber Menace if you can't feel it yourself.

# TRUST IN TRASH

Fruit, fruit, then rice. What could be more simple, no-mess and delicious? I'm very happy with this.

Fruit, fruit, rice--high as a kite. Fruit, fruit, rice and I'm in a cornucopic phantasmagoria so out of sight!

Have made the transition from plant fats to rice. It doesn't hurt and I'm thrilled to find the food so right.

I'm done with fatty acids. Since I switched to just fruit, fruit and rice I take no more Rolaids, I'm amazed.

It wasn't an avocado allergy causing pain it was fatty ACIDS cuz that's what acid does, and I'm done.

## DROP PLANT FATS FOR AWHILE

Gonna drop the nutbutters/coconut creams for awhile too, that's the fruit-FAT matrix with which I'm through.

Give it a chance to work: the HIGH SUGAR/starch/carb diet with <10% fat so the cells are cleared and fast.

Being so-called "fat adapted" was a sluggish existence tho' I thought it was great for being so delicious.

Fried white rice with onions/red bells/garlic/ginger/green onions with 1/2 teaspoon of sesame seed oil.

Fried rice is a wonderful way to conclude the day beginning with watermelon then grapefruit, what fun.

They say they've never seen me so calm. No more restless leg syndrome from wrong food in the blood.

We're afraid of the sugar when we should be afraid of the fat. I was taken into this dangerous myth against logic.

To be high as a kite the sugar must get into the cells. Fat prevents this, it covers them like a shell.

# TRUST IN TRASH

Thusly the sugar is stuck in the blood, and it's "dangerously high" as the CULPRIT of disease--a LIE.

Donald Trump is totally right--and he's HATED. Durianrider is totally right about diet--and he's HATED. Hmmmm

Tomorrow I'll have Spanish fried rice with salsa on it. Yum, what could be more delicious and a catalyst.

Without avocado I've come into the light of true perception: a proprioceptive trip from which there is no return.

## THO' A FRUIT, AVO'S A FAT

I was blocked up with green muck/slime for decades and didn't know it--avocado was a fruit, wasn't it?

They announce they're fruitarians and dive right into the avocado lure, a way to not feel hunger.

I never ate a grapefruit without an avocado. They mix perfectly but I enjoy citrus so much more now.

Arnold Ehret never mentioned avocados so we don't know--it's a modern problem with which to reckon.

They use too much olive oil too. It's splattered over everything--it's a "fruit" they keep justifying.

If you wanna overdo anything eat more starchy/SUGARY bananas and increase those types of calories.

The lowcarb crowd usually don't have the stats to prove superior health. The 811ers do, and it's swell.

The superior elite cyclists aren't fat-loading for their races, it's ALL about SUGAR--what does that tell us?

And they load STARCHES since that means sugar. It's a higher glycemic index for greater endurance.

# TRUST IN TRASH

## UNDERCARBED INSECURITY IS UGLY

It's bad when she has high expectations of him then he acts insecure and unstable being undercarbed again.

The women too are hugely disappointing when due to poor diet they vacillate like that--I'd fear em and scat.

Constant carbs will keep you steady, not up and down and what is even worse: losing confidence suddenly.

It was a false steady I felt on fats: with all the cells blocked the sugar stuck in the blood and I was a dud.

Now when I sleep it's DEEP and soothingly complete. I never slept like that on fats and dreams were murky.

In this undercarbed state they seek meat, coffee, stimulants and rely on intermittent fasting. These are signs.

I did it too man. I wasn't getting results from fruits mainly avocado so I'd intermittent fast to kick it up a notch.

High-sugar carb-up meal: cereal of your choice, rice milk, white refined sugar, optional berries. ENERGY.

## SPIN DOCTORS AND PLASTIC SURGEONS

All's a fraud in the era of spin-doctors and plastic surgeons. Superficial matters and character is lost.

It's not what things are but what they appear to be. Machiavelli

Everything depends on perceptions and what matters most is the first impression.

A very simple theory: just know the three obstructions and remove them then prepare for reward/glory.

Remove your obstruction then SNAP to your goals waiting in the wings--you're back in synchronicity.

# TRUST IN TRASH

When obstructed the personality is heavy, cluttered with nonessential/useless distractions and envy.

To succeed, eliminate the non-essential in body, mind and group. Keep the quintessential, then accrue.

Leave heaviness behind, press on to what lies ahead! Free, you're a sage or monk like stories you've read.

Rid of people problems = sage. Rid of bad habits = prosperous saint. Rid of debris =great bod in old age.

Free of sin (obstruction, missing the mark) = ecstatically happy and productive during your time on earth.

As you leave the outer/implode into the inner you'll get even more productive getting older, age no matter.

One thing I found about people is they won't weather your storms/ducking out the last hour is the norm.

## HOW TO RID JUNK AND REMORSE

How to de-clutter constantly: Into the basement put all superfluity, every six months make it empty.

You remember the event and your bad reaction to it. God remembers nothing--you just couldn't intuit.

You have character--who you are when no one sees--while the double-minded is unstable in all his ways.

Take the day to think back to all the miracles God did for you, building the faith you need for success too.

They don't want multicultural but *mono*-culture: one big (non-white) blob that *they* define and it's vulgar.

With gate locked they can't knock on your door. You might let em in and then they'd block and bore.

Character wins out/falseness fails as an overnight success crashes and hype/spin dies without leaving a trail.

## GENIUS AND CATNAPS

Not sleep and work, but nap, work. nap, work. nap, work. Catnaps revive tho' they're short.

Nap at midnight, nap in morning, nap in late aft: and productive work with music as we laugh.

Naps last for 1-2 hours usually and I'm totally ready to resume work and blow your mind see.

Its how Einstein/Picasso/Lloyd Wright did it along with all the greats: work and just catnaps.

Music is background of my life. Totally right-brained days, no politics to track my mind away.

Fruit or scampi that's my health update see and this protein I have every two or three days.

Can anything replace the refreshment of watermelon or antioxidants of pomegranate juice?

## CLIMATE ALARMISM IS COMMUNISM

Climate alarmism is a Marxist plot to undermine the west and transfer wealth to the third world fast.

It's about redistribution of wealth by soaking American taxpayers and sending it to foreign countries.

It's not just about redistributing wealth to other Americans, but to foreign nations--that's the socialist plot.

The plan by a few: planetary taxes levied by a world gov. on America because of the emissions of Co2.

# TRUST IN TRASH

A non-existent climate emergency is at the basis of Climate Alarmism. I repeat: it NEVER EXISTED, amen.

Black Lives Matter is Marxian hate dressed as racial justice and our children are being hypnotized by this.

A weakness in human nature blames others and BLM exploits that weakness to the hilt: white guilt.

Happening again: It is the embodiment of Nazi rhetoric that all Jews were responsible for the sins of one.

We see Nazi Germany as a drab, nightmarish totalitarian dystopia so of course we fear it for America.

Ask Omar next time: How are they doing with gay rights or climate change in Palestine?

The sixties were the apex of beautiful fashion for women. Sharp, chic, modest, aristocratic, smart, still slim.

## SYSTEM BASIS OF INSANITY

To liberals it's not about the crime--that's just what you pin on someone for thinking outa line.

It's a sneaky way of eliminating conservatives from public space knowing you'll get away with it.

We the deplorables are also known as the anti-woke criminals and the future looks dim ya know.

Democrats take American values away and try turning us socialist by demonizing republicans.

The fifties were an egoless generation. After what they witnessed ego was not in the equation.

One way or another wives move their husbands to the left, the most disgusting thing about the chaff.

# TRUST IN TRASH

To liberals the social is superior to independence so when I moved to the wilderness they followed me.

Yes I went crazy but at least I explored every facet of my personality and the things I'm best at see.

It wasn't your sins they were mad at, it was your politics so they used sins to buttress explanation.

The oldies are dead, the youth are gone so no one remembers you when you were down.

All they know is you lived in their town and they're proud of someone they knew when young.

## WAIT FOR THE GREAT DIVIDE

Continue your work in quiet devotion and that second arrives for your visitation/great promotion.

He said: You're under my hand now but soon I'll make your name so famous all shall know it. Jesus.

Our sins are our coping devices--its a matter of what comes first the addiction or hostilities.

You gotta wait for the nugget, the pearl. You can't force the fit/make up stuff to impress the world.

I did it for the integrity of the Creative Act & to get it out there, make it available before death.

I didn't do the Creative Act for money but my own integrity having been created to do it.

Do I feel superior to him cuz I can cue his brain in various directions? Don't be ridiculous.

I did my work under the sun, now I'll wait for God for the LINK to success and victory won.

# 100 KAREN KELLOCK BOOKS

AFFINITY OR MISERY
AGELESS CORNUCOPIA
AMERICA AWAKE!
AMERICA'S DAFT ERA
ARTS OF PALEO FASTING
AUTOPHAGY ON CHEATERS
BACKSTABBING NEUROTICS
BETRAYAL TRAUMA
BOOMERS AND BROKENNESS
BOOT ON NECK
CHAMPION GUIDES
COMMIE NUTHOUSE
COMMIES
COMMUNIST SPIRIT
CONTAGION OF MADNESS
CONTAGIOUS MADNESS
CULTURE CLASH BASHED
DAFT LEFT
DAILY FASTARIAN
DAM RATS
DIVERSITY IS CRUELTY
E-RACE WHITE
EVIL FREAKS (Beyond Gross)
THE END OR A BEND?
FEMALE BULLIES AND FEMI-NAZIS
FEMALE CARNALITY
FEMALE DUMB DOWN
FEMALE POWER DRIVE
FEMINISM AND RUIN 1 & 2
FIX FOR MISFITS
FOOLS & TRAMPS
FREEDOM SPEAKING
FRENEMY ENABLER
FRENEMY LIAR
FRENEMY THIEF
FRENEMY TRAITOR
TRENEMY TYRANT
GENIUS IS HELD DOWN
GLOBALISLAM
GOD USES THE FLAWED
HAZE OF THE LATTER DAYS

THE HERD IN WORDS
HIX POLITIX
HOW THEY RUINED US
JUST SKIP DINNER
LE FEMME AND THE COMMUNIST SPIRIT
LIBERAL CHAOS & ROT
LIBERAL DOUBLETHINK
LIBERAL GALL 1 & 2
LIBERAL SHOVE-DOWNS
LOCK YOUR GATE
LOSERS and Femme Fatales
MANUAL FOR SUPERIOR MEN
MODERN ART FROM HELL
MOSTLY FAKE
NOTES TO CHAMPS 1 & 2
OVERCOME FRENEMIES
PC MAKES US CRAZY
PEOPLE ARE CRUEL
PEOPLE PROBLEMS 1 & 2
PERSECUTED GENIUIS
POLI-PSYCH MYSTERIES
PRETENTIOUS SLOBS
QUEEN BEE
RED NEW DEAL
RETURNING TO FIRST NATURE
SEASON OF TREASON
SEPARATE MEANS HOLY
SOCIAL HYPNOTISM
SOLITUDE SOLUTION
SUPERCILIOUS
THE SCHOOLS SCREWED EM UP
TOAD TO PRINCE
TRIALS CYCLES
TRUMP VS. GROUP
TRUST IN TRASH
THE TRUTH ABOUT PEOPLE
UNDERHEANDEDLY CLEVER
WALK TALL WITHIN WALLS
WE'RE NOT ALL ONE
WINNERS SKIP DINNER
WORK OR SMERK

# KAREN KELLOCK PH.D.

M.S. Political Science, San Diego State. Ph.D. in Psychology, University of California Irvine. Postdoctoral: UCI School of Medicine, Dept. of Psychiatry [NIMH Grants]. Developed the Debris Theory of Disease, a theory of system pathology in 120 books and 22 textbooks for the general public. The theory has a general formula: All disease is obstruction, all recovery is elimination, all success is attraction. The three obstructions are people, habit and food. Remove obstruction and snap to your goals, waiting in the wings.